MISSIONS IN THE
PLAN OF THE AGES

MISSIONS IN THE PLAN OF THE AGES

•

BIBLE STUDIES IN MISSIONS

WILLIAM OWEN CARVER

M.A., TH.D.

Late Professor of Comparative Religion
and Missions, Southern Baptist Theological
Seminary, Louisville, Ky.

•

BROADMAN PRESS   Nashville, Tennessee

Copyright, 1909, by
FLEMING H. REVELL COMPANY

Copyright, 1951
BROADMAN PRESS
Nashville, Tennessee
Sixth Printing

422-127

Printed in the United States of America
2.D665

Dedicated
to the memory
of
my First Teacher in the
Bible and in Missions
MY MOTHER

PREFACE TO FOURTH EDITION

It is with deep gratitude to God that after more than forty years during which many thousands of copies have been used this study of the Biblical basis, authority and guide for missions is still in demand. The Broadman Press is assuming responsibility for a new edition through which it is expected that a new era of usefulness will be opened for this volume.

It is a surprise to the author that during all this period no other volume of such studies has been produced comparable in thoroughness and extent to his work. Through all these years the conviction has grown and received increasing confirmation that effective missionary work must be grounded in the authoritative Scriptures.

The revelation of the universal love of God and the purpose of God to provide a universal gospel for all men is the central motivation through which the Old Testament was produced, in the providence of God in creating a people designed by him to be his witnesses "among all the nations." The method of Jesus and of the Holy Spirit as his "Other Comforter" in producing the New Testament was to create a body of witnesses to the universal meaning and mission of Jesus and his gospel; and to produce the literature of the New Testament at the points and under the conditions which were brought about by the expansion of the Christian gospel in obedience to the word of the reiterated "commission" of their Lord. Every book of the New Testament was produced in this way, to solve some problem, to inspire some new activity, or to develop some new aspect of organization to answer the needs of the growing Christian movement.

It follows, therefore, that the Bible, being a product of the missionary idea and missionary work, is also the producer of missions wherever studied, accepted and obeyed. No one can understand the Bible without reading it in the missionary spirit. No one can know and believe the Bible and receive the Holy Spirit without becoming missionary.

It follows also that in principles, methods and problems of world Christianity the Bible is the true handbook of the missionary enterprise, of the individual missions and of the missionaries. It is also the missionary handbook for all pastors and churches.

It is with the conviction that an understanding of the relation between the Bible and missions will promote a new and greatly increased interest in an era of missionary expansion that the author and the publisher are sending forth this new printing of a tested study. If the author were writing a new book it would in some respects differ from the present arrangement and in a few places from the interpretation of certain Scriptures. In the main, however, the approach and the interpretations as well as the arrangement should prove satisfactory.

NOTE TO THIRD EDITION

(Excerpt)

The most important study of missions is the study of the Bible. It is a source of gratitude that God is pleased to use this volume of studies of His Work in His Word. The author recognizes that so full a study of missions in the Bible—wherein some seven hundred passages are treated at greater or less length—is too elaborate, and calls for too much serious study and reading, for the average study class to use all the work as it stands, or for the average reader to follow the entire line of study. He ventures to hope, however, that by proper handling the work is readily available for study classes of college students, young people's societies, women's societies and laymen; and that any interested Christian may here find the Biblical idea of missions so presented as to be grasped without undue effort.

PREFACE TO FIRST EDITION

(Excerpt)

The work proceeds upon the assumption of the Divine origin and validity of the Scriptures in detail as well as in general. The author quite agrees with those who think that not all the work of Biblical criticism can rob the Bible of its missionary character so long as any part of it remains, since missions belong to its very essence. It cannot be denied, however, that in practice as well as in theory, missionary workers come most largely from the ranks of those who accept the Bible in a sense quite different from that of the radical criticism. This work does not hesitate to quote and expound individual passages as authoritative while it recognizes fully the worth of the appeal to the general spirit of the whole Word.

The foundation principles of the Christian task of the world conquest are to be found in the Bible, not so much in the authority of an imposed duty as in the impulse of the spirit of our Religion, the genius and the very life of our Faith.

It is these fundamental principles that the author has sought to present from the Word.

In the main the text of the American Standard Revision has been used, but where required for clearness or proper emphasis the author has not hesitated to render the original in his own phraseology.

CONTENTS

Missions in the Plan of the Ages

I

THE MISSIONARY IDEA IN THE BIBLE

I. DEFINITION

MISSIONS mean the extensive realization of God's redemptive purpose in Christ by means of human messengers. *acting under the guidance of the Holy Spirit.*

It is not possible closely to mark missions off from other work in that kingdom of God which it is ever the first duty of every disciple to seek. It will be suggestive to say that missions introduce the kingdom of heaven which other work deepens and develops in the extent and power of its influence in the whole life of man. Missions is the proclamation of the Good News of the kingdom where it is *news;* further evangelization and ministration make manifest the *goodness* of the news, emphasizing and applying it in the varied relations of our life. It is too common an error to mark off by geographical lines missionary work from other phases of evangelization.

Jehovah is "the Judge of all the earth"[1] and

[1] Gen. 18 : 25.

"His kingdom ruleth over all."[1]   God's ideal includes all this and more. As expressed in the Christ it is that His kingdom shall rule *within* all. It is the spiritual ideal, wherein all shall know God, from the least to the greatest.[2]   The Divine Logos was in the world and the world was made through Him and yet the world did not know Him. He was indeed the true Light lighting every man who comes into the world; and yet as the Life-light of men He shines in a darkness that not only fails to "apprehend" the Light, but even resists and seeks to "overcome" it.[3]   Missions is the agency through which the people that walk in darkness come to see the Great Light and by which the Light shines upon them that are dwelling in the land of deep darkness.[4]

We shall see how fully the Scriptures teach that for this age the Father and the Son have appointed missions as the process for approaching the ideal of God's spiritual reign on earth.

II. ORIGIN

1. The origin of missions is *ultimately* to be found in the heart of God.   His are the redemptive purpose and plan.   No thought of God is true to His revelation of Himself that does not rest on the fact that He "so loved the world that

[1] Ps. 103 : 19.　　　　　　[2] Jer. 31 : 34.
[3] Cf. John 1 : 10, 4 f.　　　[4] Isa. 9 : 2; cf. marginal reading.

He gave His only begotten Son" that by believing in Him "the world should be saved through Him." [1]   It was God that was "in Christ reconciling the world unto Himself, not reckoning their trespasses unto them;" [2] and not so reckoning for the reason that this love-sent Son "is the propitiation for the whole world." [3]   This attitude of God is eternal and is determinative in all His dealings with men.   He is ever working towards the end that "they who have not heard" may have "the glad tidings preached unto them"; that "they who were no people may come to be a people of God's own possession." [4]   So it is that when men come to be God's "ambassadors on behalf of Christ" they must go to all ignorant and erring men beseeching them "to be reconciled unto God." [5]

In our time this missionary idea of God is playing a large part in saving our theology and vitalizing it with a new life.

Modern missions more than all else have fostered the true idea of the Father love of God for sinful and incomplete men.   In speculative theology two imperfect views have been in sharp conflict.   One school has insisted on the judicial interpretation of God, to be moved in behalf of man only by the bloody persuasion of a crucified

Schools *①*

---

[1] Cf. John 3 : 16, 17.   [2] 2 Cor. 5 : 19.
[3] See 1 John 2 : 2, original.   [4] Isa. 52 : 15; 1 Pet 2 : 10.
[5] 2 Cor. 5 : 20.

Christ. In this view God meets Christ for man only on Ascension day. Another school, as narrowly speculative as the first, interprets God sentimentally and finds the Christ practically serviceable for impressing men but not essential to man's redemption. The theology of missions—the theology that produces missions and is fostered by missions—interprets God as revealed in Christ: "God was in Christ reconciling the world unto *Himself*."[1] It is missions that have done most, although, it may be, largely indirectly, to give currency to this conception of God, so vital in the Christianity of our time. It is sometimes thought that the Old Testament view of God is more largely judicial. But we must remember that in the Old Testament the Redeemer is not very clearly distinguishable from Jehovah God, and when a "Daysman" does stand between man and God he comes from Jehovah and as the Servant of Jehovah to redeem His people—all people. In the one Old Testament passage where the Redeemer is the Son of Jehovah this sonship is of the essence of Jehovah. The Old Testament bears elaborate evidence that God moves in universal love to men for centuries before He is manifest as Immanuel—God-with-us. Such is the theology of missions which take their rise in the heart of God. An exclusively "forensic theology" hindered the beginning of modern mis-

[1] 2 Cor. 5 : 19.

sions ; an exclusively sentimental theology hampers the progress of missions.

2. The *historical* origin of missions is found in the work, the life, the command of Jesus Christ projected in the lives of His followers. Like every other " fact of Christ" missions have foundation and preparation in the prior history of God's dealing with men, recorded in the Old Testament. How abundantly this is true we hope in some measure to set forth in these studies. The culmination of the preparation for, and the historical beginning of, God's out-reaching for a lost world, as contrasted with what we may call His previous down-reaching, are to be found in the Christ.

In the fact of incarnation there lies already the implication of race conquest. And since God *incarnation.* has become man to bring men to God it must be that as men become identified with this redeeming God they will extend and hasten His endeavor.

As the Light enlightens men they must themselves shine forth as luminaries among men.[1] In the Prologue of John's Gospel [2] there is the clearest identification of the Word with the entire race of men, and not with any one section of it. His preincarnate relations are presented with no limitations but with the most emphatic universalism. To be sure in His earthly life the Logos comes to " that which was His own " ; but there is immedi-

[1] Cf. Phil. 2 : 15; Matt. 5 : 14.   [2] John 1 : 1-18.

ately revealed a deep contrast between this providential and potential ownership and that vital and actual ownership which alone He recognizes. Those of His own that received Him must have His "authority to become children of God," and as such children need a nature "not of blood, nor of the will of the flesh, nor of the will of man, but of God." "The Word became flesh," not Jew, nor Greek, nor Barbarian, but essential humanity. Again we read, "No man hath seen God at any time," Jewish man and Greek man included without distinction ; and to all classes "the only begotten Son who is in the bosom of the Father hath declared Him."

Missions mean that every one who comes to the bosom of the Son, and so to the knowledge of the Father, in his turn also declares Him to mankind.

Various events connected with the advent of the Son of God, in the infancy of Jesus, proclaim the universalism of His mission. In the records of Matthew and Luke in the midst of simple-hearted Jewish people, cherishing the best elements of a too narrow Messianism, we seem to be moving in an atmosphere of universalism. The conscious concepts of Zecharias and Joseph, of Elizabeth and Mary, of the shepherds and of Anna may well enough have been limited to Jewish redemption ; but they were spiritual conceptions and as such must needs express themselves in terms that most readily lead to universal appli-

cations. In these days of the Son of God to
express their thoughts angels and men drew on
the prophets of universal Messianism, Daniel and
Isaiah, and the Messianic psalms. Mary discerns
that in her Son God will fulfill His word of
" mercy towards Abraham and his seed forever," [1]
a word which God, certainly, meant to include
blessing for all mankind.

The Angel Chorus [2] was of a universal peace,
however it seemed to the shepherds. Simeon, by
special warrant awaiting the sight of the Lord's
Christ, when he held Him at length in his arms,
blessed God and said :   *Praise God !*

". . . Mine eyes have seen Thy salvation
Which Thou hast prepared *before the face of all*
peoples,

A light for revelation to the Gentiles
And the glory of Thy people Israel." [3]

He puts first the "revelation to the Gentiles,"
reversing the order of Isaiah, in both 42 : 6 and
49 : 6.   In the visit of the Magi and their worship [4]
there is universalism, in the fact itself, in the necessary antecedents of the fact and in the inevitable
consequences of their visit and the knowledge
with which they returned to their own lands.

The work of Jesus, although technically limited
to " the lost sheep of the House of Israel," [5] never-
theless constantly transgressed current Jewish

---

[1] Luke 1 : 55.   [2] Luke 2 : 14.   [3] Luke 2: 30–32.
[4] Matt. 2 : 1 ff.   [5] Matt. 15 : 24.

ideals and in some examples, at once prophetic and characteristic, went beyond the limits of His assigned mission. Thus was His work true to the essential universalism of its spirit, a spirit that did not, because it could not, fail to impress all classes in His own generation. Jesus aroused the enmity of His opposers, the suspicions of His friends, and the hopes of the aliens, that in His thinking and work man, and not Jew merely, was the aim.

In the teaching of Jesus, both in its general terms and principles and in specific precept, He laid the foundation for, and enjoined upon all His followers, universal missionary work. Leaving details for later exposition it will be sufficient now to note the general facts. The Jewish leaders had more than an instinctive feeling that in the word and work of this Teacher lay the germs of a universal love and aim incompatible with, and destructive of, exclusive privileges for themselves and their nation. It was in large measure His liberalism that inspired their hatred and urged them on to accomplish His death.

Jesus' favorite designation of Himself was "Son of Man." His choice may well have been influenced by the fact that this was the characteristic Messianic term. That it identified Him with every man and all men was a stronger reason and was also the explanation of the employment of the term by the prophets. Jesus has ever in mind the needs of man when He interprets the Law, the traditions, the obligation of the Sabbath, His own message, and His death that will draw all men unto Him.

Son of Man

It is in the effort of His followers to interpret their Master's mind that we have the four Gospels which set forth the universal Gospel distinctly conceived to be aggressively designed for all humanity.

3. The *practical* origin of missions. If ultimately missions arise from the heart of Him who is "Lord of all and rich unto all that call upon Him;"[1] if historically missions begin in the life and word of the Son of Man who is come to seek and to save that which was lost; continuously missions spring from the very spirit of our religion. In its very essence Christianity is a propaganda. It goes forth for conquest in the name of its Lord. The Christian is full of loving concern for men and emptied of selfish aims. In a world of need he is a channel of supply; in a world of darkness, himself some time darkness, he is now light in the Lord[2] and must illuminate the darkness; in a world of death he is an agent of Life.

The Christian life is a life begun and sustained by the Holy Spirit. But the Holy Spirit is first of all the witness-bearer of Jesus the Redeemer.[3] It cannot but be that Christians, too, bear witness when they know Jesus. Whenever Christianity

Holy Spirit

[1] Rom. 10: 12.   [2] Eph. 5: 8.   [3] John 15: 26; 16: 13 f.

has been true to its origin and faithful to its spirit, wherever it has been spiritual—marked by the Spirit's presence—it has been crying, in the wilderness, of the kingdom of God come among men. There is no separation of the missionary impulse from a true and vital Christianity. The antecedent conditions, the initial facts, the continuous experience of any one into whom the life of God has come all move him to make known his Saviour.

III.   THE TEXT-BOOK OF MISSIONS

For the student in the theory of missions the Bible is the text-book. Here is the record of the preparation for the kingdom of heaven, its principles and its progress. Not that the story of the kingdom is to be found only here. Had the history of the race and of its nations and tribes been written from the same standpoint as the Scriptures all would be an account of the unfolding and development of God's plan of Redemption for all men by the Man, Christ Jesus. For indeed " all history is just His story." [1]   The child of the kingdom is free thus to read history and for such a reading the returns are great. For such reading the missionary study of the Bible is the preparation. The principles set forth in the Bible find illustration and elucidation in the stories of the nations. In a special degree is this true also of the history of Christianity, in its achievements and its failures,

[1] Dr. A. T. Pierson.

in its allegiance to the spirit of the Master and its
lapses from the ideals of His kingdom. Ecclesiastical history should properly be a study of missions.

In the history and the practice of missions various
theories of missions arise which are to be tested
and corrected by the principles found in the Bible.
It will not fall within the plan of these studies to
present and discuss the various theories except
incidentally or as they vitally affect the teaching
of the Word of God. These studies will not con-
tend for but aim to exhibit the Bible teaching concerning missions.

In the Bible as the missionary text-book we find,
characterizing its general spirit and emphasized
in definite passages, the missionary thought in
God's heart, the missionary message in Christ's
atonement, the missionary duty in our Lord's
commands, the missionary motive in the nature of
the redeemed life, the missionary task in a "world
lying in the evil one," [1] the missionary power in
"the Holy Spirit whom God hath given to them
that obey Him," [2] the missionary goal in "the day
of Jesus Christ." [3]

When we designate the Bible the text-book of
missions we mean to affirm more than that the duty
and plan of missions may be found in the Bible.
They must be found there in any true and ade-
quate reading of the Word. Jesus grounded in
the Old Testament, as well as in His own direct

[1] 1 John 5 : 19.   [2] Acts 5 : 32.   [3] Phil. 1 : 6.

authority, the universal scheme of religion which He presented to His followers and the realization of which He entrusted to them. Paul and the other Apostles appealed to the sacred Scriptures in support of their course and their ideals in seeking to save all men and make them subject to the will of God in Christ Jesus. The answer to Jewish narrowness was the Jews' Bible.

If the Old Testament furnished our Lord grounds for His plans and commands to conquer the world in His name, all the more is the New Testament missionary. It is first of all a product of the missionary work of the early Christians and it was produced primarily to meet the needs of this work.

Acts

What else is the Book of Acts than an inspired account of first experiences in executing the commission under the impulse and guidance of the Holy Spirit? What Jesus "began"[1] to do in His personal ministry He continues in the person of His disciples under the power of His Spirit. The introduction to Acts tells how the Ascension hour message of Jesus was: "Ye shall receive power when the Holy Spirit is come upon you; and ye shall be My witnesses, both in Jerusalem, and in all Judæa and Samaria, and unto the uttermost part of the earth."[2] The Book then occupies itself with telling of the coming of the power of the Holy Spirit and of the witnessing commanded by the

[1] Acts I : I.   [2] Acts I : 8.

Master, with its results. Thus Acts constitutes the first chapter in the story of Christian missions, their inauguration and early progress.

When and why were the Gospels written? When the extent and conditions of witnessing to Jesus made it impracticable longer to rely on the verbal accounts concerning Him to whom the missionaries gave their witness: to preserve the true message and to make it accessible to reading men the evangelists committed to writing "those things which had been fully established" upon the testimony of "them who from the beginning were eye-witnesses and ministers of the Word." [1]

Mark, first of all, wrote "An Introduction to the Good News of Jesus Christ, the Son of God." [2]

By recording facts from the life of Jesus and comparing them with Old Testament prophecies Matthew proves that Jesus is the Christ of God. His aim is not alone to prove that Jesus is the Messiah of Jewish hope but that He is the Messiah of the Divine promise and plan, a much larger meaning.

Luke gives a universally adapted account of the character and work of the Son of Man setting up God's kingdom in men to take possession of the world.

John wrote when the Apostolic interpretation of Jesus was questioned. He wrote among Gentiles for the needs of a missionary work already

[1] Luke 1: 1f.   [2] The correct rendering of Mark 1: 1.

world-wide. He takes from his knowledge of the earthly life of the Lord a few critical, characteristic incidents and teachings for the announced purpose "that the readers might be led to believe that Jesus is the Christ, the Son of God; and that in this belief might have life in His name." [1]   So the Gospels are all missionary tracts setting forth the Gospel that its conquests might be extended and its work confirmed.

Of the "General Epistles," James is for the instruction of the mission converts in the righteousness of the Gospel; 1 and 2 Peter and Jude are to encourage the mission converts under persecutions and to secure their faithful adherence under adverse circumstances; 1 John is designed to show the grounds of assurance in Christ in the face of corrupting theories of sin by which the converts of the second half of the first century were beset; 2 John most probably to commend and warn a mission church; 3 John is to encourage and approve a brother who in a church that opposed missionary work had worthily supported the missionaries even under penalty of excommunication.

Paul's epistles were all called for by the needs of his missionary labors to follow up the work he had begun; to maintain the purity of the Gospel against corruptions in doctrine and life; to defend his own missionary apostleship against

[1] John 20 : 31.

the assaults of the Judaizers; to expound the universal principles of the Gospel; "to reprove, to rebuke, to exhort, with all long-suffering and teaching," [1] the children whom he "had begotten through the Gospel." [2] Three of his letters are addressed to younger missionaries to give them warning and instruction for their work "that they might speak the things befitting sound teaching" and "commit the same to faithful men who should be able to teach others also," and thus to secure the perpetuity of the work. [3]

Paul's letters

Hebrews is a missionary apologetic for meeting the hindering contentions of the Jewish religion, and is a marvellously well-adapted document for use among Catholic peoples in our day, as well as a fine illustration of the true method of dealing with any religion which must be met and supplanted by Christian missions.

Hebrews

The Revelation belongs to the time when the terrible Roman persecutions were seeking to destroy the results of the first generation of missionary labors. It is full of encouragement for the time and of prophecy of the outcome of the proclamation of "the everlasting Gospel." [4]

Revelation

If there had been no commission, or no obedience to its spirit, there would have been no need for the New Testament writings and no occasion for their production. A product of missions, the

---

[1] 2 Tim. 4: 2.   [2] 1 Cor. 4: 15.
[3] Cf. 1 Tim. 6: 20f.; Titus 2: 1, 2; 11 Tim. 2: 2.   [4] Rev. 14: 6.

New Testament can be truly interpreted only in the light of the missionary idea.

If our view of the Bible's relation to missions is correct it will manifestly be impracticable to set down and expound every passage containing or affecting the missionary enterprise. Nor is that needful. We shall undertake to follow the great ideas of Scripture teaching upon this subject, presenting them by means of quotation or reference and with exposition of characteristic passages.

II

THE MEANING OF MISSIONS TO GOD—THEIR AUTHOR

WE have laid stress on the fact that God is the Author of missions. World-wide redemption is not an afterthought but a part of the eternal purpose of the Heavenly Father. God's relation to this idea and its execution will appear more emphatically as we inquire what missions mean to God.

1. First of all we read that missions is *the method by which God is now carrying forward His "plan of the ages."* Let us turn here to Ephesians 3 : 1–13. At this point the Apostle a second time in this epistle comes to record a prayer for the saints in Asia. " For this cause," he says. " This cause " is set forth in chapters 1 and 2, wherein the plan of God for world-wide redemption is wonderfully set forth, showing how " now in Christ Jesus ye that once were far off are made nigh in the blood of the Messiah. For He is our peace who made the two one by destroying the fragment-making wall, enmity, when in His flesh He rendered inoperative the law of commands merely dogmatic " : and this with the end " that the two (great divisions of the race) He might in

27

Him (Christ) create into one new humanity, making peace. And (the prior and further fact) He would reconcile both elements in the one body (the new humanity) to God by means of the cross." [1]   For men who had in themselves the work and the witness of this reconciling Messiah Paul will pray now, as he has prayed already. But wait a moment!   This prayer has to do with eternal ideas and everlasting issues. We shall not yet hear the petition.   The Apostle will make sure that his readers enter into the spirit of his prayer and so he will again, and more specifically, set forth the ground on which such a prayer is to be offered.   Hear him: " If indeed you grasped the content of the dispensation of God's favor which was given to me with reference to you, that by revelation was made known to me the secret (so remote was it from the thought of men that God must bring it to us by special word) as indeed I wrote briefly a bit ago, by referring to which (see Ch. 1 : 3–14, especially 11–14) you can see my insight into the secret of the Messiah, the secret which to other generations was not made clear to the children of men as now it is uncovered by the Holy Spirit for His holy Apostles and prophets : the secret being that the Gentile peoples are an inheritance jointly, a part of the body and joint participants of the promise which is contained and realized in Christ Jesus by means

[1] Eph. 2 : 13 ff.

of the Gospel message ; of which Gospel I came
to be a minister by the free gift of God's grace,
bestowed on me in accordance with His mighty
energy. To me, then, the less than least of all
saints, was given this grace, to the peoples to proclaim in my Gospel the immeasurable wealth of
the Messiah and to bring the light of true interpretation upon what is the real mission of the
secret that from the ages preceding has been
hidden in God, the Creator of all things ; that
mission being that now, at length, by means of
His Church God's remarkably varied wisdom may
be made known to the principalities and authorities in the heavenly spheres. All this revelation of
God's covered wisdom in the dark problems of
hopeless peoples in sinful ages, now illuminated
by the open secret of a universal love in a glorious Gospel for all, is in exact accord with *a plan
of the ages*, which (plan) God made in His Messiah, Jesus, our Lord, in whom we have boldness
and access—in our universal undertaking—in the
confidence of His faith. So I ask you not to be
in distress over my suffering tribulations over
you Gentiles (heathen), for it is your glory to have
such a Gospel and I can readily suffer to reveal
this glory."

Having made such an explanation as a basis for
its intelligent comprehension, Paul now comes to
resume the prayer—itself briefer than the exposition of its ground (verses 14-21). The prayer we

shall study later.   Let us now briefly examine the words preparatory to the prayer.

Paul takes the common New Testament position that "God constructed 'the ages' in Christ."[1]   The plan on which God is constructing these ages— epochs in His world drama—has been concealed from even the highest intelligences in heavenly relationships.   Now the Messiah has come, with reference to whom and by whose active agency all is made and moved.   And to the missionary apostles and prophets the key to this plan is now revealed.   It is not a "mystery" in the sense of being complicated and difficult of apprehension. Rather its very simplicity has been in part its obscurity.   The key to understanding all God's dark dealings through the ages is simply a universal love going out in redemptive purpose.   Jesus had expressed it in His life and in that sentence radiant with revealing hope and glory : "God so Loved the World that He Gave His Only-begotten Son that Whosoever believeth in Him might not perish but have Everlasting Life."   To Paul God had, in grace, given special discernment into the wonderful, universal bearings and implications of this key-secret to God's ways, now put into the hands—aye the hearts and heads, of all who will come after Jesus Christ.   What he has heard in the ear the Apostle now peals forth from the housetop.   His way of stating "the secret" is

[1] Heb. I : 2, Greek.

that the Gentiles share in God's thought with the Israelites in being God's inheritance, Christ's body, recipients of Messianic promise. This he will have all men see while heaven's people look on in admiring wonder.

Paul perceives that in Gentile Christians lies the hope of comprehending, and of applying too, for this is vastly important, the universalism of the good news of God's love. So he makes this prayer for, and this appeal to, Gentile Christians. In Romans [1] Paul tells us that this is a detail of the plan of God.

The preaching of the Gospel to all men means much to God. The progress of His age plan in Christ Jesus depends upon it. Another age—it may be other ages—are to follow this of missionary proclamation of the Christ to all men. The next age waits on the completion of this. God's vindication for allowing a world with sin, before "the principalities and powers in the heavenly relationships," depends upon the outcome of this age wherein is to be made known to the peoples the wealth of the Messiah, which God declares, by Paul, to be past tracing out. Missions mean much to God.

2. Missions is *a method by which God will realize the end of His dealing with the nations and tribes of men*. This is, to be sure, but another way of looking at "*the plan of the ages*." **Here**

[1] Rom. 11 : 11-36.

we have to do with the historic growth, the political development, the ethnographical distribution of men.

The success of the missionary work is essential to the proper outcome of God's control of the peoples of the earth. This control is a constant assumption of the Bible and finds frequent assertion. It has always been necessary—still is needful—that men remind themselves that God has never deserted any class or race, nor abrogated His claim to them, nor surrendered His control over them. This truth is to be seen alike in God's general providential dealings with men and in the facts and history of the Elect Race. After all, the chief difference between Israel and other peoples is twofold: (1) in the purpose for which God used each people in His plan, and (2) the manner of writing the histories. Israel's history is written from the theocratic standpoint and would read very differently if written from the " secular " viewpoint, as so many would seem to prefer to have it written. So also would the history of Greece, of Babylon, of Rome, of England, of America read very differently from our present reading of it if we had it written from God's standpoint by a historian by inspiration made competent to interpret God's hand and heart in the careers of these peoples.

Paul states the principle here involved in Acts 17 : 22-31. Speaking to the cultured but idolatrous Athenians, the Apostle recognizes their re-

ligiousness as a basis of appeal for true religion
(22), finding in their "Altar to an Unknown God"
a blind groping after "the God that made the
world and all things therein, the Lord of heaven
and earth" (23–24), whose true relation to all men
the Apostle proceeds to teach: "He Himself
giveth to all life and breath and all things; and
He made of one every race of men to dwell upon
all the face of the land, having marked off seasons
appointed for them and the assigned limits of their
habitation, for them to seek the God, if, in this providential arrangement they might, indeed, feel after
Him and find, while to be sure He remains, from
the start, not distant from each one of us; so near
in fact that in Him is our living, our activity, our
very existence, a truth announced by some of your
own poets, where we read, 'For we are also His
offspring'" (25–28).

Paul concludes against idolatrous conceptions of
God (29), and returns to his main theme; "God,
being such in nature and relations to men (οὖν)
overlooked the times of such ignorant worship
and preserved you to the present time and conditions (τὰ νῦν) wherein He commands men that
they shall all everywhere repent inasmuch as He
has set a day in which He is meaning to judge
the inhabited world in righteousness in the person and standard of a man whom He designated,
furnishing to all an assurance of this by raising
this man from the dead" (30–31).

Note the Apostle's claims : (a) All men have a religious sense leading towards God, even when He is unknown ; (b) God is the maker of all and is not to be worshipped materially as if in need for He gives to all men all that they have including life and its activities and powers ; (c) God made all men of a common stock and has in all a common interest, concern and control ; (d) The control of God over men extends to a determination of the time and place they occupy in the history of the world of nations, and to intimate, supporting presence with each individual ; (e) The purpose of God in these relations to men is that they may seek Him, feel after Him, find Him ; (f) Because God's purpose is such He does not destroy men while in ignorance they are making false steps in the worshipful search but comes at length to meet them, as in this case, by the missionary, with clear revelation of the Gospel ; (g) God now lays on men, all, everywhere, the call to repentance, enforcing it with the menace of a righteous judgment in Jesus Christ whose resurrection from the dead is assurance to all men of the fact that this call, and its judgment-warning, is from God.

There can be no question that Paul here puts all men on the same basis before God and affirms most strongly that God is the God of all men, has never deserted any class or race, has not abrogated His claim to any, has not surrendered His control over any, and that the good news of His seeking men in the Saviour is intended for all, as also is the warning of the judgment.

Application of this principle to the missionary enterprise abounds in the Scriptures. Perhaps it is most abundant in Isaiah where it constitutes one of the characteristic features of that Book. In the first part it appears in the "Burdens" of the nations, in the predictions of the Son to be born for universal rule, and in numerous specific statements that foreigners shall share the blessings of redemption. In the second part the promises and prophecies concerning the servant of Jehovah, the words of cheer to the desolate Israel, the visions of the new heavens and the new earth are at every turn made to include all who shall learn faith among all peoples, and they shall be very many. As examples of such teaching we may read 44 : 24–45 : 25, where all phases of Divine control, general and particular, are affirmed and the end, salvation offered to all, distinctly set forth ; 60 : 1–14, where Zion is called to "Arise, shine" upon the darkness of the nations who will come to her light, and a glorious vision is presented of the multitudes coming from all the ends of the earth ; and again 66 : 18–24, where we read that God takes knowledge of men's works and thoughts, He will gather all nations and tongues to witness His glory and will set among them a sign ; that such as are saved will be sent to declare God's glory among the nations that have not yet heard His fame

nor seen His glory, and that when these missionaries bring their "brethren out of all nations" "of
them also will I take for priests and for Levites,
saith Jehovah." When priests and Levites are
taken from all the nations it will mean that the
people of these nations have come to worship
Jehovah. That missions—the proclaiming among
all men of the kingdom of God—is the end of
God's dealing with the nations is evident in the
teaching concerning both general providence and
election. Possibly there is less of essential distinction between providence and election than we
usually think.

Besides the typical passage, already studied, in
Acts 17, Paul has an instructive, almost startling,
passage in Galatians 4 : 1–9. "But I say for so long
a time as the heir is a minor child he differs nothing from a bond-servant, though lord of all ; but
is under the control and care of guardians and
household stewards until such time as is designated
by his father. So in the case of us Jews—children of the promise that we were—there was a
childhood period when we were as slaves under
the training of the elements of the world—leading
a life that, except for its hopes, was the same with
that of all natural men. Then when the training
period was completed and God's right time came
He sent out His one real Son to have a human
birth and a life, like ours, under law in order that
He might redeem us who were under law so that

we should receive our sonship. Now while we, Israelites, were in the position of a minor son you, Gentiles, were in the position of a slave—the two positions being, remember, in no wise different. And in the fullness of time you, too, have been made sons. And because ye are sons God has sent out the Spirit of His One Son into our hearts (Jews' hearts, Gentiles' hearts, all alike, and so our hearts), crying, this Spirit of God's Son in us, Abba, Thou Father. So that thou art no longer slave but son, and if son also heir through God. It is through God in the case of both. But then, during the slave days, you, because you did not know God, enslaved yourselves to them that in their nature are not gods, though you took them for such. But now that you have made God's acquaintance, or rather, as we have seen the truth to be in the case of us all, since you have been recognized by God, how are you turning back again to the poor sickly elements such as belong to minor sons and to which you would but be in another bondage?"

One nation was in the condition of a minor son while the rest were as servants in the house, but all were alike in the mind of God. To all there came "the fullness of the times" when in God's redeeming plan God took knowledge of them, recognized them as ready for sonship. At this stage the Son of God came in person to the son-race and came in the Gospel of His Son to all the races,

and as they are sons sends forth the Spirit of His
Son into our hearts to teach us to address our
God as the Father. Such is Paul's teaching of
God's plan with the races of men. On this princi-
ple Paul proceeded in his own labor as we see,
for example, in Acts 13 : 46–48.

As Paul in this last instance found in Isaiah the
ground for his teaching we may well turn to that
prophecy also. Among many statements setting
forth this teaching look at three:

Isaiah 56 : 1–8. The righteous must hold fast to
their faith and courage " for My salvation is near
to come, and My righteousness (near) to be revealed. . . . Neither let the foreigner that
hath joined himself to Jehovah, speak, saying,
'Jehovah will surely separate me from His people,' " thinking that even if allowed to worship and
blessed in the worship they must still expect God
to give them a position subordinate to the Chosen
People. Not so, but " also the foreigners that join
themselves to Jehovah, to minister unto Him, and
to love the name of Jehovah, .   . will I bring
to My holy mountain, and make them joyful in
My house of prayer ; . . . for My house shall
be called a house of prayer for all peoples. The
Lord Jehovah, who gathereth the outcasts of Israel,
saith, Yet will I gather others to him to be added
to Israel's own that are gathered."

Isaiah 66 : 18–21. " It shall come to pass that
I will gather all nations and tongues ; and they

shall come and see My glory." The method of doing this is described: "I will set a sign among them and such of them as escape by this sign will I send unto the nations, . . . and they shall declare My glory among the nations." All the redeemed shall be one, for these missionaries "shall bring all your _brethren_ out of all the nations. . . . And of them also will I take for priests, for Levites, saith Jehovah." Priests and Levites from all nations speak significantly of nations sanctified and worshipping Jehovah.

Isaiah 51 : 4–5. Jehovah's Servant has accepted His humiliation and set Himself for suffering, for judgment, for salvation (50 : 4–11). The work has begun with hope in Israel (51 : 1–3). Now " Attend unto Me, O My peoples ; and give ear unto Me, O My nation ; for a law shall go forth from Me, and I will establish My justice for a light of the peoples. My righteousness is at hand, My salvation is already gone forth to do its work, and Mine arms shall judge the peoples." So comprehensive is this plan and work that not only will it embrace the populous lands but even " the isles shall wait for Me and put their reliance on Mine arm." The coming of the Christ is God's plan for each people whose life He maintains on the earth. They wait for Him.

The goal of God's dealing with the nations will receive new emphasis if we examine it in relation to the national election of the Hebrew people.

How these people themselves interpreted their election will be examined elsewhere and does not here concern us. What did God mean by it? is now our question.

First of all let us see this election in its origin, Genesis 12 : 1–4. " Now Jehovah said unto Abram, ' Get thee out of thy country, and from thy kindred, and from thy father's house, unto the land that I will show thee ; and I will make of thee a great nation, and I will bless thee, and make thy name great ; and be thou a blessing ; and I will bless them that bless thee and him that curseth thee will I curse ; and in thee shall all the families of the earth be blessed.' So Abram went as Jehovah had spoken unto him." In the second verse Jehovah gives a threefold statement of the promise to bless Abram and then solemnly commands him : " And," by consequence and as the end of your blessing, " be thou a blessing." He must by the measure of this " great nation " and " great name " and " blessing " bless others. He is separated from other men to become a source and centre of blessing for all men. The idea and the command are now enforced by a new form of statement in verse three : " I will bless them that bless thee." Their blessing will come in their seeing, appreciating and responding to the Source of your blessing. " And him that curseth thee will I curse." Abram will then become, and his posterity, the standard for judgment among men. Through them will God make known His character, in blessing and in curse, among men. And the outcome: " In thee shall all the families of the earth be blessed." It is idle to try to obviate the Messianic meaning of this call to Abram by rendering this last climactic assurance "shall bless themselves" and then limiting its significance to a sort of vague form of pronouncing or perceiving blessings. Besides the unworthiness of such an idea, it has no fulfillment in fact and could not have been expected to have any. God called Abram and Israel to be the channel of a race redemption. We shall see how this idea was reasserted to each of the Patriarchs.

Turn now to Exodus 19 : 3–6. The newly-made nation stands just across the Red Sea that buried their day of bondage and upon the threshold of a national history. God calls Moses to Mount Sinai to get the law of the nation's life. Hear His very first word : " Jehovah called to him out of the mountain, saying, ' Thus shalt thou say to the house of Jacob and tell the children of Israel : Ye have seen what I did unto the Egyptians, and how I bare you on eagles' wings, and brought you unto Myself. Now, therefore, if ye will obey My voice indeed, and keep My covenant, then shall ye be Mine own possession from among (or above) all peoples : for all the earth is Mine ; and ye shall be unto Me a kingdom of priests, and a holy nation. These are the words which thou shalt speak unto the children of Israel.' " Note how solemnly this first message from the mount is introduced and ended. How brief a message it is! And how significant! The law of the national life, religious life, social life is not yet given.

First let Israel get her bearings. First let the people learn the reason for their separate existence. Let them hear the meaning of their past preservation and their future career. It was God who had acted on them and on the Egyptians. He had brought the children of Israel, not to Canaan, not to glory, but "to Himself." Now their future as peculiarly His own people will depend upon their obeying genuinely His voice and keeping His covenant—covenant inherited through Abraham and to be made anew with the nation. Such was His character and such His plan with Israel that only thus could He afford to make them His special own, above all peoples, as they reflected His character and manifested His glory among men. They must not forget that all the earth is His and all its peoples. If He takes this one tribe to His heart for the time it is not to forget the rest but to do good to all. His aim is that Israel shall serve Him as a kingdom of priests, a nation set apart to prophetic service. But when the priest and the prophet are a nation, the people for whom they minister and to whom they prophesy are the other nations. Abraham's call lies at the basis of Israel's election in the plan of God.

Did the nation miss the function of its priest-

hood and forget to be holy among the people until destruction overcame them and they faced a
decimating captivity, because Jehovah's plan and
purpose were not served by them? Must Jehovah
declare unto them: " Thy first father sinned, and
thy interpreters (who should have made thee see
the meaning of thine election) have transgressed
against Me. Therefore will I make the holy
princes profane and I will make Jacob a curse,
and Israel a reviling "? [1] Yet is there an elect
within the Elect, who will be Jehovah's chosen
servant. To this servant Jehovah has yet a message. Isaiah 44: 1–8: " Fear not O Jacob My
servant ; and thou Jeshurun whom I have chosen.
For I will pour water upon the thirsty land and
streams upon the dry ground. I will pour My
Spirit upon thy seed, and My blessing upon thine
offspring." What result will follow this outpour-
ing of the Spirit in blessing? Why " they shall
spring up among the grass, as willows by the
watercourses," and in all parts be eager to own
Jehovah. " One shall say, I am Jehovah's ; another shall call out by the name of Jacob ; and another write his name down as belonging to Jehovah and take on Israel as a surname," exactly
as happens every day under the missions of the
Gospel.

How shall it come about? Jehovah, the King
of Israel, the Redeemer, Jehovah of Hosts, de-

[1] Isa. 43 : 25–28.

clares to this elect few who thirst for Him and wait for Him that He alone is God, first and last (verse 6), but will have some who, in His stead, "shall call, and shall declare it and set it in order for Me" (the history of His revelation of Himself), "since I established the ancient people;" and these representatives of Jehovah must "declare the things that are coming, and that shall come to pass" (verse 7). For this work the discerning elect are ready: "Fear ye not, neither be afraid; have I not declared unto thee of old and showed it?" Have no fear for the future since My word has been fulfilled in the past and is fulfilled in you who stand before Me to-day, "And ye are My witnesses." "Is there a God beside Me? Yea, there is no Rock; I know not any" (verse 8). So you must proclaim Me to the peoples that are without God. This relation of the faithful ones to Jehovah and their function in His plan, appear strongly stated in Isaiah 43 : 8–13.

National priesthood is taught clearly also in Isaiah 61 : 4–6. Already in Isaiah is it appearing that the priestly, prophetic people, God's true Elect, are something more than, and other than, a political entity among the nations and the "people for God's own possession" appear in their true light in the New Testament. Their function remains the same, more clearly understood, and in their new capacity they are free to discharge this function, as they could not be while national hopes and national

needs hampered.   Peter takes up exactly this idea
of election and applies it to the Christians in
1 Peter 2:9–10: "Ye are an elect race, a royal
priesthood, a holy nation, a people for especial
ownership, in order that ye may announce out
from yourselves the excellencies of Him who called
out of darkness into His marvellous light; you
who formerly were a no people (of God) but now
are God's people, who were those who had not
obtained mercy, but now have obtained mercy."
The Apostle proceeds to exhort that this "peculiar
people" shall have their "behavior seemly among
the heathen peoples," so that by beholding the behavior of the people of God, these "may glorify
God in the day of visitation."

Once again does the function of collective election appear in the vision of the Lamb taking the
Book of God's redeeming plan from the Father's
hand to open its seals before the hosts about the
throne (Rev. 5). "And when He had taken the
Book, the four living ones (forces of nature) and
the four and twenty elders (representative redeemed ones from Israel and from the Gentiles)
fell down before the Lamb. . . . And they
sang a new song, saying: Worthy art Thou to
take the book and to open its seals; for Thou
wast slain and didst purchase unto God with Thy
blood men of every tribe, and tongue, and people,
and nation and madest them to be unto our God
a kingdom and priests; and they reign upon the

earth." Then when the whole universe has joined a chorus of praise to the Lamb, "the four living ones said, Amen. And the elders fell down and worshipped" on account of the revelation and of the Revealer and the Executor of the plan of redemption, *viz.*, the taking of some elect from among all peoples and making them the head of the whole race to bring in the blessings of Jehovah upon all.

3. Taking a further step, completing the view of God in the nations and in the race, we find, in the *third* place, that missions are *God's method of bringing humanity to its ideal, its destiny*. This will have appeared in some of the passages already studied and is involved by the whole spirit of God's message. God moving in humanity must bring humanity to its destiny, and God makes known His presence and His ends among men by the preaching of the Gospel. In the vision of the Lamb we were just now studying (Rev. 5), when "the living ones" and "the elders" had sung their new song of the redemptive plan then "ten thousand times ten thousand, and thousands of thousands" of angels joined in another song of praise; "and every created thing which is in heaven and on earth and under the earth, and on the sea, even all things that are in them" John heard saying, "Unto Him that sitteth on the throne, and unto the Lamb be the blessing, and the honor, and the glory, and the dominion, unto

the ages of the ages." This plan, now revealed, would perfect God's work of redeeming and subjecting all in harmony unto Him forever.

When "the Word became flesh and dwelt among us, full of grace and truth" (John 1 : 14) our humanity had its seal of sanctification to a divine destiny to be realized when of the race it can be said " For of His fullness we all received and grace upon grace" (John 1 : 16).

We have seen already how in His own body as the unifying agent and ideal our Christ will build up of redeemed men of all ages and lands a spiritual body that will constitute under God a " new humanity" (Eph. 2 : 15).

The closing vision of the Book of Isaiah (66 : 22–24) is of "the new heaven and the new earth" which Jehovah will make, and as they " shall remain before Me, saith Jehovah (as the goal and end of My work among men) so shall your seed and your name remain (as the centre and agency through which the new order is brought forward). And it shall come to pass (with this ideal and this seed ever before Jehovah) that from one new moon to another, and from one Sabbath to another, shall all flesh come to worship before Me, saith Jehovah. And they shall go forth and look upon the dead bodies of them that have transgressed against Me, for their worm shall not die, neither shall their fire be quenched ; and they shall be an abhorring unto all flesh."

For when all is done that men will allow by the testimony of the Gospel God's punitive power will expel from the body of the living all the rebels. Now let us keep in mind that this final word of "the Evangelical Prophet" follows immediately on his vision of a universal missionary campaign, employing missionaries from all lands to declare Jehovah's glory among the nations (verses 18–21).

John's vision of "a new heaven and a new earth" (Rev. 21–22) is significant for that its inhabitants are men, not angels and seraphs. The New Jerusalem is not above to which men are carried but " comes down out of heaven from God " and is heralded with the announcement, " Behold the tabernacle of God is with men and He shall dwell with them and they shall be His peoples (plural) and God Himself shall be with them, their God." [1] We are not now undertaking to set up any theory of the order of events marking the close of the Gospel age and bringing in the new age of glory. Of that we shall see in the last chapter. What we here read from the Word is that " According to God's promise we look for a new heaven and a new earth wherein dwelleth righteousness." [2] This is God's ideal for the human race and so its destiny. The delay to consummate this end by the might of His power is due to God's patient love towards men, "not

[1] Rev. 21 : 2–3.   [2] 2 Peter 3 : 13.

wishing that any should perish, but that all should come to repentance." [1] It is God's call to us who "look for these things to give diligence that we may be found spotless and blameless in His sight" and to draw the right practical conclusion that the <u>patient delay of</u> our Lord has for its meaning the extension and completion of His salvation, "even as our beloved brother Paul wrote unto us, according to the wisdom given him." [2] Paul has touched upon this point in many places. Peter's reference is perhaps to Romans 2. Bearing more specifically on our present point is the passage in Romans 8 : 19–22. The passage is an incidental, illustrative argument in a longer paragraph [3] dealing with the full sanctification of believers in Christ. As explaining, in a way, the glory to be uncovered ultimately upon believers we read : " For the dear desire and expectation of the creation (the goal of the world-making) awaits, for its realization, the uncovering of God's sons. For the creation was brought under the present madness, because of a hope that even the creation itself shall be freed from the slavery of corruption and delivered into the freedom of the glory of God's children : the subjection not being a willing one but accomplished through Him that subjected it." This present "natural order" so full of apparent disorder as to seem to be under vain law or lack of law is part of a process to a glorified

[1] 2 Peter 3 : 9.   [2] Cf. 2 Peter 3 : 14 f.   [3] Verses 18–25.

creation. But the new order cannot come until God's sons have been disclosed, made manifest, out of and in the midst of the disorder. How Paul expected this to be accomplished is partly set forth in the marvellous argument[1] from which our passage is taken; partly also by his own labors and teachings to bring all men to a knowledge of the truth. He "endured all things for the elect's sake that they too may obtain the salvation which is in Christ Jesus in the midst of the eternal glory."[2]

In beginning the missionary campaign committed by the ascending Lord to His followers, when the Holy Spirit had come upon them with the promised power, Peter's first word in the new undertaking, in explanation of the remarkable conduct of the believers, was the announcement that this was the fulfillment of God's word by Joel,[3] and so inaugurated a campaign in which God would pour forth of His Spirit upon all flesh, an era in which salvation will be offered, upon faith, to all classes and peoples; "whosoever shall call upon the name of the Lord shall be saved."[4] Whether Peter comprehended the full import of the prophecy, the first chapter of whose translation into history he was now opening, does not signify. In obedience to the command of Christ and by the impulse of the Holy Spirit he was

[1] Rom. 5–8.
[3] Joel 2: 28 ff.
[2] 2 Tim. 2: 10.
[4] Acts 2: 14–21.

inaugurating a method by which God was moving towards His goal for humanity.

Finally, of God's destiny for men read the Eighth Psalm and study its interpretation in Hebrews 2. Indeed may we say: We see not yet all things subjected unto man but we see Jesus, identified in all things with human men, whom He now calls His brothers and for whom, every man of them, He has tasted death; we see Him " for the suffering of death crowned with glory and honor," and " through death bringing to nought him that hath the power of death, that is the devil, that He may deliver all them who through the fear of death were all their lifetime subject to bondage." [1]

4. *Missions* thus appear to be *the message of God's love to men*. One of the significant features of heathen religions is their failure to conceive of the love of their gods. Apart from the Gospel this is also largely true of the religions of Jehovah, Judaism and Mohammedanism. They serve with the bondage of the letter, not with the freedom of the spirit. There were many in Israel through the centuries who rose to the evangelical idea of a God who loves good men and chosen men; and some even had a dim idea of God's love for bad men—the only kind, as the truth is about men. Jesus revealed the heart of the Father and told, in many a parable, of a love that goes to seek and to

[1] See Heb. 2: 9 ff.

save that which was lost. He spoke of the shepherd seeking the one lost sheep out of a hundred, of the woman in grief until the lost coin lay again in her box, of a father rejoicing over the home-coming of a prodigal son and grieved that the brother did not share the joy. All of which Jesus repeatedly declared means that there is joy in the presence of the angels over one sinner that repenteth. That "in the presence of the angels" means in the Father's heart.

Jesus pitched His ministry and His mission on the fact that He was here because "God so loved the world that He gave His only begotten Son" and was careful that His disciples should not think of the Father as less loving than Himself. It was out of the Father's bosom that Jesus came, and abiding in that bosom of the Father He revealed God. The law could be given through Moses ; grace and truth came through Jesus Christ.[1]

We are not now thinking of what God's love means to men but of what men mean to God's love. Missions is the method by which that love revealed in Jesus is made known to the race. This is God's way of reconciling the world unto Himself. That going out of God after sinning, ignorant men is a conception of Deity found nowhere outside an evangelistic, missionary Christianity   Only two other religions are at all mis-

[1] Cf. John 1 : 17 f.

sionary and neither of these has the least conception of bearing a love message from the Father-God.

Isaiah 55 is truly interpreted only as a universal call of a God of tender compassion. The proffered covenant is "the sure mercies of David" whom Jehovah had "given for a witness to the peoples, a leader and commander to the peoples" (verse 4). (Note the plurals.) Nations are now to be called and will run unto Jehovah's Servant "because of Jehovah thy God, and for the Holy One of Israel; for He hath glorified thee" (verse 5).

Paul shows how "when we were yet weak at the opportune moment Christ died in behalf of men ungodly. For scarcely for a righteous man will one die, yet for the good man some one, perhaps, might dare to die. But God commendeth His love towards us in that while we were yet sinners Christ died for us." [1] God commendeth His love to us sinners! "But God being rich in mercy, for His great love wherewith He loved us even when we were dead through our trespasses," [2] is another statement of that fact basal to the missionary idea and work. "God, our Saviour, would have all men to be saved and come to the knowledge of the truth." [3] The missionary must labor and strive because he has his hope set on the living God who is the Saviour of all men. [4]

[1] Rom. 5: 6-8.
[4] 1 Tim. 2: 4.
[2] Eph. 2: 4.
[3] 1 Tim. 4: 10.

He is therefore long-suffering towards men " not wishing for any to perish but for all to come to repentance." [1]   This wish of God sent His Son to the world and sends the Gospel of His Son to the uttermost parts of the earth.   " Herein is love, not that we love Him but that He loved us and sent His Son as the propitiation for our sins," " and He is the propitiation . . . not for our sins alone but also for the whole world." [2]   This, then, is one meaning of missions, God's chosen way of revealing His love to a world that is in the death of sin ; and because God's love wants this sinful world.

5.   One other thought of the significance of missions to God ; they are *God's way of fulfilling His eternal promises to His Son.*   Other methods He will use, but for this age and for our religious duty this is the method, most clearly commanded, most practically available and most universally applicable to all Christ's followers.   God is at work through all the civic and social forces of men and in ways we know not.   Increasingly is He employing men to introduce the evangelistic, missionary idea into " secular " tasks, so that men " seek first the kingdom of God " in many spheres. This is a restoration of the early Christian ideal of the use of the missionary method.   It is in such inclusive sense we use the term.

Turning now to the Second Psalm we find in it four clearly marked sections.   The first three

[1] 1 Peter 3 : 9.   [2] 1 John 4 : 10.

verses sketch a vivid picture of the raging, rebellious nations. "Jehovah and His anointed"
clearly claim the right of rule over them all and
their claim is known and resisted. This is the
righteous rule of the moral God and Maker of
men that they seek to cast aside.

The next three verses speak of God's attitude
towards the rebellious people. He could well afford to make sport of their vain ravings and im-
potent rebellions (4); but He will not leave them
alone but will rebuke them for their sin and bring
them into trouble through their sin (5); then He
cannot leave them so for He has a purpose of
righteous love and His honor must be saved even
among these sinners and so He declares: "yet,"
in spite of their violent resistance, and of the necessary visitation of wrath,

"Yet I have (in plan and decree) set My King
upon My holy hill of Zion" (6). There shall yet
be a rule of righteousness, holiness among men.
Beyond the nations' sins and Jehovah's wrath lies
the reign of holiness.

Verse 6 has spoken of the reserve counsel of
God. This will now be more fully presented in
three verses:

"I will tell of the decree;
Jehovah said unto Me, Thou art My Son;
This day have I begotten Thee.
Ask of Me and I will give the nations for Thine
inheritance

And the uttermost parts of the earth for Thy possession.

Thou shalt break them with a rod of iron ;

Thou shalt dash them in pieces like a potter's vessel."

Did the devil have in mind this promise of eternal decree when he offered our Lord at the beginning of His work " all the kingdoms of the world and the glory of them " ? Surely Jesus spoke out of the consciousness of this eternal promise when He said, " All authority is given unto Me in heaven and on earth. Go ye therefore, and make disciples of all the nations," and " Ye shall be My witnesses . . . unto the uttermost parts of the earth." And so Jesus seems clearly to have seen that the Father's gift was to be realized in conquest through His missionary witnesses. This method is also implicit in the last three verses of our Psalm, where a gracious invitation and appeal is extended to the rebels to " serve Jehovah with fear," " to kiss the Son " and " take refuge in Him " for after a time the anger will be kindled and the work be consummated by power.

The Twenty-second Psalm in the first twenty-one verses sets forth the sufferings of the Messiah, while the remaining verses speak of His acceptance of His mission. At verse 27 the vision becomes extensive :

" All the ends of the earth shall remember and turn unto Jehovah ;

All the kindreds of the nations shall worship before Thee.

For the kingdom is Jehovah's ;
And He is the ruler over the nations."

When Psalm 72 tells of "The Reign of the Righteous King," some expressions are used which no writer could imagine exhausted in Solomon or any other king, or even applicable to any human king, as verses 5, 17, and, hardly, 8, 11. When applied to the "greater than Solomon" they hold a worthy meaning and a measured promise.

For repeated statements of this promise one has only to turn to Isaiah. The Servant shall suffer but "He shall see of the travail of His soul and shall be satisfied : by the knowledge of Himself shall My righteous Servant make many righteous."[1] More specifically in 42 : 1–13 do we follow the promise. Jehovah " upholds Him," " delights in Him," "puts His Spirit upon Him," "He will bring forth justice to the nations," He will deal gently with all true faith, "He will not fail nor be discouraged until He have set justice in the earth ; and the isles (even) shall wait for His law" (verses 1–4). So far Jehovah speaks about His Servant. Now (verses 5–9) He turns to speak to Him. First He describes Himself in power and authority : then, " I, Jehovah, have called Thee in righteousness, and will hold Thy

[1] Isa. 53: 11.

hand, and will keep Thee, and give Thee for a covenant of the people, for a light of the nations ; " then follow details and new assurances.

It is in chapter 49 that we come to the most definite of all the promises. Here the Servant Himself speaks and outlines His experiences in a way marvellously parallelled in the career of Jesus and His followers. Hear Him : " Listen O isles unto Me ; and give heed ye peoples from far (all the world is called to hear): Jehovah hath called Me from the womb ; from the bowels of My mother hath He mentioned Me by name (and signified the (My) character) for He hath made My mouth like a sharp sword ; in the shadow of His hand hath He hid Me (so that His use of Me was not foreseen) : and He hath made Me a polished shaft (devoting special care to Me as the chief weapon of His plans) in His quiver hath He kept Me close (as precious and to be reserved for just the right crisis in His warfare). And He said unto Me (the account drops the figure and becomes personal), Thou art My Servant ; Israel (Prince of God), in whom I will be glorified." But in the actual experiences the Servant seems to find these promises failing : " But I said, I have labored in vain, I have spent My strength for nought and vanity (How often might it well have seemed so to our Lord in His days on earth and since) ; yet (I must not give up, nor lose faith—must " not fail nor be discouraged ") surely the justice due Me is with Jehovah, and My recompense is with My God." God had promised success in the enormous work. It comes tardily. God has an answer for His Servant, for in spite of appearances Jehovah is in Him and honors Him : "Yea, He saith, It is too light a thing that Thou shouldst be My Servant to raise up the tribes of Jacob and to restore the preserved of Israel (I mean to go quite beyond that with you): I will also give Thee for a light to the nations, that Thou mayest be My salvation unto the ends of the earth. Thus (further) saith Jehovah (to) Israel's Redeemer, His Holy One, to Him whom men (now) despise, whom His own nation abhors, and who is for the time subject to earthly rulers : Kings shall come to see who and what He is and shall arise unto Him ; princes, too, shall worship Him ; because Jehovah, who hath chosen Him, will keep faithfully His promise, even the Holy One of Israel (the Covenant-maker of the ages)." How Jesus understood all these promises and applied them to Himself ; how His life and the career of His kingdom correspond to the promises ; how He laid His plans and gave His commissions in accordance with these words we are learning more and more. Missions is the plan by which He expected His Father to fulfill the promises and it is the method by which God is to-day filling up the measure of the hopes of " the travail of His soul " until He "shall be satisfied."

III

THE MEANING OF MISSIONS TO JESUS—THEIR FOUNDER

WHAT God hath eternally planned as one great stage in His redemptive working Jesus inaugurated. In His own person He revealed the attitude of God towards men in a sinful world; in His death He made atonement for the world and framed the most powerful appeal within the power of God; in His words He gave the message for all men and in His authority He provided that faithful witnesses shall tell the good news "to earth's remotest bounds." We must seek to see in some measure how the missionary age and plan seemed in His eyes.

1. Jesus saw as His own work and the mission of His missionaries *the revealing of the Father unto the world.* "The word became flesh and dwelt among us and we beheld His glory, glory as of the only begotten from the Father."[1] "No man hath seen God at any time, God only begotten, the Son, who is in the bosom of the Father (and who therefore knows God as the Father) He hath manifested the Father." Now came "grace

[1] Cf. John 1 : 14, 18.

and truth." God can never be understood until He is known as Father.

The prayer of the kingdom of heaven must be addressed to " Our Father." [1]   The ideal of life for the kingdom is, " Ye therefore shall be perfect as your Heavenly Father is perfect." [2]   All the worship of the kingdom must be for the eye of " your Father who seeth in secret." [3]   The children of the kingdom are to be free from care because " your Father knoweth that ye have need of all these things," and so you are ever to " seek first His (the Father's) kingdom and His righteousness." [4] We are bold in prayer for, " If ye then, being evil, know how to give good gifts unto your children, how much more shall your Father who is in heaven give good gifts unto them that ask Him." [5] And it is because you sustain, in His kingdom, such a relation to the God of the kingdom that you can afford and are bound to observe, " All things, therefore (N. B.), whatsoever ye would that men should do unto you, even so do ye also unto them." [6]

Jesus was careful to keep before men this character of revealer of the Father. " Jesus cried and said, He that believeth on Me, believeth not on Me, but on Him that sent Me. And He that beholdeth Me beholdeth Him that sent Me. I am come a light unto the world, that whosoever be-

---

[1] Matt. 6: 9.   [2] Matt. 5 : 48.   [3] Matt. 6 : 4, 6.
[4] Matt. 6: 32 f.   [5] Matt. 7 : 11.   [6] Matt. 7 : 12; cf. 5 : 11

lieveth on Me may not remain in the dark. . . .
For I spake not from Myself; but the Father that
sent Me, He hath given Me a commandment,
what I should say, and what I should speak. And
I know that His commandment is life eternal; the
things therefore which I speak, even as the Father
hath said unto Me, so I speak." [1] When the Jews
rejected His word and person, Jesus took refuge
in the hope that when they had " lifted up the Son
of Man" they would know that He was the true
representative of His Father. [2] If His disciples had
gotten to know Jesus, they would have known
His Father too: " And from henceforth ye have
known Him, have even seen Him."   Philip spoke
more truth than he knew when he said, " Lord,
show us the Father and it will satisfy us."   Jesus
knew exactly that to know the Father was the
satisfaction of the world's hunger. "Jesus saith
unto him, Have I been so long time with you and
yet hast thou not known Me, Philip? He that
hath seen Me hath seen the Father; how sayest
thou, Show us the Father?   Believest thou not that
I am in the Father and the Father in Me," [3] and He
makes a touching appeal for faith in the Father
through Himself.   It is because He goes to the
Father that the disciples can do greater works
than the Master Himself has accomplished.   So
Jesus presses home on the hearts of His missionaries that their life and work all relate to the

[1] John 12: 44-50.   [2] John 8: 28.   [3] Cf. John 14: 6-12.

Father.[1]   Then He makes them understand that
" as the Father sent Him, even so sends He them "
to reveal the Father unto the world.[2]   Jesus felt
that His work was complete when He had manifested the Father's name unto the men assigned
to Him and made them keep the Father's word
and know that of a truth Jesus had come forth
from the Father, sent by Him[3] and His lament for
the world is that it has not known the righteous
Father.[4]   In their work Jesus will insist that His
missionaries remember that "times and seasons
the Father hath set within His own authority."[5]
Jesus knew Himself to be the Son whom His
Father, having appointed Him to be the heir of
all things, sent to speak unto us ; the effulgence
of God's glory, the impress of His substance, who
having made purification of sins, sat down at the
right hand of the Majesty on high.[6]   His commission to make disciples of all the nations looked to
the revealing of His Father to all men—for the
Father's sake first of all.   Through missions Jesus
makes the world know His Father.

2.   Another phase of our Lord's conception of
His mission, continued in His missionaries, was
*to glorify His Father's name by taking away from
among men the blasphemy and dishonor of that
name* in heathenism, idolatry, irreligion.   Prophet

---

[1] Cf. John 14–16.

[2] John 20 : 21 and cf. 17 : 18.

[3] Cf. John 17 : 6–8.

[4] John 17 : 25.

[5] Acts 1 : 7.

[6] Heb. 1 : 2–3.

and psalmist in Israel had been taught the jealousy
of Jehovah from the day of Moses. " He would
not give His glory to another, nor His praise unto
graven images." [1]

The first table of the law, emphasizing and
guarding the honor and glory of Jehovah's name
lay at the foundation of all religion of spirit and
life in the Word of God.   No preparation so fitted
for prophetic leadership as did the vision of the
holiness of God and of the withholding of the
honor due His name by sinful peoples.

Polytheism and idolatry were not merely foolish, bringing the worshippers into confusion and
shame, but were an insult to the one God and a
robbing Him of His rightful praise.   All sin of
heart and conduct was a profanation of what God
would have sanctified and was an offense unto the
holiness of Him who " could not look upon sin."

When the Messiah came He found Himself in
the midst of a race profaning the house of His
Father, the religion of His Father, the world of
His Father, the name of the Almighty God.   He
opened and closed His ministry by symbolical
cleansings of the Temple in Jerusalem and His
disciples, shortly to become His first missionaries,
remembered that it was written, " Zeal for Thine
house shall eat Me up." [2]   And the word in the
Psalm quoted [3] continued, " And the reproaches of
them that reproach Thee are fallen upon Me."

[1] Isa. 42 : 8.   [2] John 2 : 17.   [3] Cf. 69 : 1.

Jesus could not fail to see Himself set to fulfill the prediction that " the glory of Jehovah shall be revealed, and all flesh shall see it together, for the mouth of Jehovah hath spoken it " ; [1] words that close the paragraph applied by the Baptist to himself as " the voice of one that crieth in the wilderness." In that clearest of all prophetic outlines of His mission, Jehovah said to the Coming One, " Thou art My Servant; Israel (Prince of God) in whom I will be glorified." [2]

Jehovah had taken note of the ways of men, " For I know their works and their thoughts ; it shall come to pass that I will gather all nations and tongues ; and they shall come and shall see My glory ; " [3] and so it was that Jehovah would make the place of His feet glorious when He should glorify the place of His glory. [4]

It was in accord with this magnifying of the glory of Jehovah's name that the Messiah's advent was heralded by an angel choir singing

" Glory to God on high
And on earth peace." [5]

The outcome of the Messiah's work is pictured in the hosts that swell the universal chorus,

" Holy, holy, holy, Lord God Almighty." [6]

The first word of petition in the prayer Jesus

[1] Isa. 40: 5.   [2] Isa. 49: 3.   [3] Isa. 66: 18.
[4] Isa. 60: 7.   [5] Luke 2: 14.   [6] Rev. 4: 8; cf. Isa. 6: 3.

teaches His disciples to pray is : " Our Father
who art in heaven, hallowed be Thy name."
These words are not, one fears, generally taken at
the value our Lord put upon them.   Indeed one
has found many who did not account them a petition at all but an ascription of praise.   Jesus taught
us thus to pray that the Father's name may be held
holy on earth as it is in heaven.   This was the
first, the fundamental, step in the coming of the
kingdom of God upon earth, wherein God's will
shall be done even as it is in heaven.   If men shall
sanctify the name and person of the Heavenly
Father and apply the meaning of that holiness the
time will have come when " there shall be upon the
bells of the horses, HOLY UNTO JEHOVAH ; and the
pots in Jehovah's house shall be like the bowls before the altar.   Yea every pot in Jerusalem and in
Judah shall be holy unto Jehovah of hosts ; and all
they that sacrifice shall come and take of them,
and boil therein ; and in that day there shall be no
more a Canaanite in the house of Jehovah of hosts." [1]

In the Sermon on the Mount where Jesus teaches
this initial petition of the children of His kingdom,
He has set forth the comprehensive duty of these
children of God ; " Let your light shine before men
as a city set on a hill that cannot be hid, or as a
lamp on a lampstand shining to all that are in the
house that they may see your good works *and
glorify your* Father who is in heaven." [2]

---

[1] Zech. 14 : 20–21.   [2] Matt. 5 : 14–16.

All through His ministry Jesus was powerfully moved when He saw the godlessness of the people.   He was especially indignant with the Pharisees whose proud selfishness expelled the spirit of worship from their own souls and made them hindrances to the glory of God among their people.

So it was that Jesus came to the close of His labor still burdened for the glory of His Father among men.   When Judas went out from the upper room to complete the betrayal Jesus comforted Himself with the assurance that " Now is the Son of Man glorified, and God is glorified in Him." [1]

In laying before His own their labor Jesus says, " Verily, verily I say to you, He that abides in faith upon Me the works that I do that one too will do ; and greater than these will he do, because I am going before My Father ; and (in the prosecution of this work) whatever ye may ask in My name (for My work) that I will do in order that My Father may be glorified in His Son." [2]   When He urges His followers to abide in Him as branches in the vine and assures them that, so abiding, they may ask whatsoever they will and it shall be done, it is that " *Herein is My Father glorified*, that ye bear much fruit, and ye shall be My disciples." [3]

So comes our Lord to the end of all His labor " and lifting up His eyes to heaven, He said, Father the hour is come ; "—the prophetic hour,

[1] John 13 : 31.   [2] John 14 : 12-13.   [3] John 15 : 7-8.

the pivotal hour of history and of the kingdom, the hour for which the world waits and on which it depends, the hour that is to justify the creation of man; what will He say?—"glorify Thy Son, that the Son may glorify Thee. . . . I glorified Thee on the earth by finishing the work which Thou gavest Me to do."[1] So comes He to the end eager for the glory of the Father. This is the task He commits to missionaries under the Holy Spirit. Surely now "His own whom the Father gave Him out of the world" will "Declare His glory among the nations, His marvellous works among all the peoples"[2] and "All nations whom Thou hast made shall come and worship before Thee, O Lord; and they shall glorify Thy name."[3]

3. *By missions Jesus will bring in the kingdom of heaven upon earth.* This is the form in which Jesus seems most constantly to have conceived His work and so the work of His witnesses. Of course the kingdom concept dominates the pre-Christian revelation, reaching its most definite expression in such Messianic passages as Isaiah 9, Daniel 2, etc.

"For unto us a child is born, unto us a son is given; and the government shall be upon His shoulder; and His name shall be called Wonderful Counsellor, Mighty God, Father of Eternity, Prince of Peace. Of the increase of His government and of peace there shall be no end upon the

[1] John 17: 1-4.   [2] Ps. 96: 3.   [3] Ps. 86: 9.

throne of David, and upon his kingdom, to establish it and to uphold it with justice and with righteousness from henceforth even forever. The zeal of Jehovah of hosts will perform this." So Isaiah. Daniel is more detailed in the famous dream of the progress of the kingdoms of history: "And in the days of those kings shall the God of heaven set up a kingdom which shall never be destroyed, nor shall the sovereignty thereof be left to another people; but it shall break in pieces and consume all these kingdoms, and it shall stand forever" (verse 44). In the time of Daniel, if not long before, it came to be common to refer to God as the everlasting King:

"Thy kingdom is an everlasting kingdom, and Thy dominion endureth throughout all generations." [1]

It was altogether in accord with this teaching that John the Baptist came preaching in the wilderness, "saying, Repent, for the kingdom of heaven is at hand." [2] And that Mark's record [3] runs: "Now after John was delivered up, Jesus came into Galilee, proclaiming God's good tidings and saying, The time is fulfilled, and the kingdom of God is at hand: repent and believe in the good tidings."

Such was the burden of the preaching of John and of Jesus: the primary petition of our prayers

[1] Ps. 145 : 13; cf. Dan. 4 : 34, etc.   [2] Matt. 3 : 1–2.
[3] Mark 1 : 14–15.

is that God's kingdom may come, and this too must be the first effort of the follower of Jesus always. In prayer and effort we must put the kingdom before our food and raiment, before our personal protection and care, before every other thing.[1]

There are three recognized groups of parables in our Lord's teaching, given at three epochs in His ministry. The subject of them all is the kingdom of heaven; its founding and growth;[2] its principles and progress;[3] its consummation and glory.[4]

The kingdom of God may then be said to be the formative concept of Jesus' ministry. It was this He commanded His disciples to preach;[5] this He promised His disciples when the "little flock" must be encouraged;[6] this He confessed before Pontius Pilate He was in the world for;[7] and He declared as the plan of His campaign that "these good tidings of the kingdom shall be preached in the whole inhabited earth for a testimony unto all the nations; and then shall the end come."[8]

What the end may imply Jesus leaves to Paul to suggest: "Then cometh the end when He shall deliver up to His God and Father the kingdom, when He shall have abolished all rule and

---

[1] See Matt. 6: 9 ff., 33.   [2] Matt. 13, etc.
[3] Luke 10–13, etc.   [4] Matt. 25, etc.; Luke 20, etc.
[5] Luke 10: 9 ff.; Matt. 1c : 7.   [6] Luke 12: 32.
[7] John 18: 37. The words of Jesus involve this.   [8] Matt. 24 : 14.

all authority and power . . . then shall the
Son also Himself be subjected to Him that did
subject all things to Him, that God may be all
in all." [1] Paul claims also that there is " made
known unto us the secret of God's will, according
to His good pleasure which He planned in Christ
for a dispensation of the fullness of the times, to
sum up all things in Christ." [2]

In missions, then, Jesus is bringing to the world
" God's good message of the kingdom."

4. We think it is evident also that *Jesus looks
upon missions as the projecting of Himself forward
unto a sort of complete self-realization.* He was
incarnate for the race of mankind.   If the value of
that incarnation is dependent upon believing acceptance by man, then in a true sense the incarnation is incomplete until all men are made aware
of it and accept or reject its meaning for their
lives.   We do well to make much of the second
coming of our Lord, but let us remember that for
millions of His and our fellow men, our Christ has
as yet had no first coming and that He looks to us
to effect by a missionary Gospel this primary incarnation.   The thought is a daring one.   But
was not this in His mind when our risen Lord at
the first meeting with His followers in the barred
room " says to them, Peace to you.   And on saying this He showed both His hands and His side

[1] I Cor. 15 : 24–28.
[2] Eph. 1 : 8 ff.; cf. Phil. 2 : 9 ff.; Col. 1 : 14–20.

to them. The disciples rejoiced, therefore, on seeing the Lord. He said therefore (in light of their
joy of recognition) to them again, Peace to you,
as My Father sent Me so also do I send you.
And on saying this He breathed on them and says
to them, Receive the Holy Spirit : whosesoever
sins ye remove, they are removed for them, and
whosesoever ye retain, they are retained." [1]

This explains, too, the much controverted words
to Peter, and to the rest, in Matthew 16 : 19,
wherein Jesus gives to His followers the keys of
the kingdom of heaven, to bind and to loose on
earth for heaven.

So far did Jesus identify Himself with His servants that He looks upon a typical case of the
world's need and exclaims : "We must work the
works of Him that sent Me while it is day ; the
night cometh when no man can work." [2]   "We"
—you, whom I have called to carry on My work,
and I. Luke had in mind this idea of the Lord
when in beginning Acts he refers to " the former
treatise of all that Jesus began to do and to teach," [3]
recognizing that Jesus continues doing and teaching in His Spirit-filled followers. How this
thought moves the mind of our Lord in the night
of His passion we shall presently see.

5.   As in the case of the Father, so also of the
Son do we find that *missions are His expression
of love and sympathy for a lost world.*

[1] John 20: 19–23.   [2] John 9: 4.   [3] Acts 1 : 1.

This love for the lost, for man as man and as possible son of God, was with God's Son a passion that marked Him among all in the day of His flesh and that calls the world to marvel in all time. Early in His ministry, in Samaria, where aliens and enemies to His Jewish blood fell under His spell, and again when the shadows were long on the brief day of His personal ministry, and now in Judæa where He was most unwelcome, did the hungry, misguided hearts of men appeal to Jesus as a white harvest calling for many laborers.[1]

No incident could be more truly characteristic of Jesus than that recorded in Matthew 9 : 36–10 : 5, and it illustrates exactly the idea here emphasized : "When He saw the multitudes He was moved with compassion for them, because they were distressed and scattered as sheep not having a shepherd. Then saith He unto His disciples, The harvest indeed is plenteous but the laborers are few. Pray ye therefore the Lord of the harvest, that He would send forth laborers into His harvest. And He called unto Him His twelve disciples, and gave them authority over unclean spirits to cast them out, and to heal all manner of disease and all manner of sickness.   .   These twelve Jesus sent forth.   .   .   ."

Satan had, in the great temptation, sought to appeal to Jesus by showing Him all the kingdoms of the world and the glory of them—as masses, in

[1] John 4 : 35 ; Matt. 9 : 37 f. ; Luke 10 : 2.

splendor, to be exploited for Himself. In the Holy Spirit He saw all the men of the world and the misery of them and Himself to relieve that woe. Into this world that hated Him and would hate them, Jesus sends His disciples whom He has taken out from the world. " He had compassion on them ; " " Then He saith unto His disciples : ' There is a great, wasting harvest, Pray, Go.' " That was another characteristic and parabolic scene, recorded by all four Evangelists, when Jesus fed the five thousand. " He came forth and saw a great multitude, and He had compassion on them . . . and He began to teach them many things. . . . But He answered and said unto them, Give ye them to eat." He teaches, and He feeds, but His compassion commands in this service all who are His. His sympathy and His power provide the food, but " He gave the loaves to the disciples, and the disciples to the multitude." [1] The disciples must ever be the hands through which the heart of the Redeemer lays hold on needy men.

The Saviour who weeps in longing over persistently rebellious Jerusalem is the same Jesus who declares " Other sheep I have which are not of this fold. Them also I must lead." [2] The world stood before the eye of His love and He said, " God sent not His Son into the world to condemn the world but that the world should be saved through

[1] Matt. 14 : 19.   [2] John 10 : 16.

Him;"[1] and again, "I am come a light unto the
world, . . . for I came . . . to save the
world."[2] It was when Greeks came desiring to
know Him that the Lord said, "The hour is come
that the Son of Man should be glorified. . . .
Now is a judgment of this world; now shall the
prince of this world be cast out. And I, if I be
lifted up from the earth, will draw all men unto
Myself." And it was as part of this same teaching
that He laid down the law of spiritual life: "Except a grain of wheat fall into the ground and die
it abideth by itself alone; but if it die, it beareth
much fruit. . . . If any man serve Me let
him follow Me; and where I am there shall also
My servant be; if any man serve Me him will
My Father honor."[3] Thus did Jesus include all
His servants in His redemptive work and see the
Father honoring Him in them and drawing all
men unto Him. It was enough. For this hour
had He come into the world.

In the prayer with which Jesus completes His
sacrificial life and from which He goes through
Gethsemane to His humiliation we have all these
items of the meaning of missions crowded together
in the wonderful words in which He presents His
life and its issue in the world before the Father.
We must close this chapter with a study of this
prayer: John 17. We submit an outline of the
prayer from this standpoint and believe that this

[1] John 3:17.   [2] John 12:46 f.   [3] John 12:20–33.

will appear to be the actual line of thought followed by the Lord. There are thus three divisions with a gradual transition from one to another so that in each case the transition verse will belong to both the preceding and the following section.

(1) Jesus presents Himself to the Father, with His work accomplished and asks for its acceptance and for glory (verses 1–8). But His work has resulted chiefly in getting a small band of understanding believers and these come before Him and now (2), He lays them before the Father in earnest petition (verses 8–20). Praying for these, His own, brings forward the world in which Jesus is leaving them, and (3), the last section makes an earnest cry for the world that lieth in the wicked one (verses 20–26).

Now we shall examine these sections somewhat in detail. " These words spake Jesus," words that have set before His disciples what they are to expect, to be, to accomplish, to suffer in the world, concluding, " In the world ye have tribulation ; but be of good cheer ; I have overcome the world." [1] " And lifting up His eyes to heaven," bringing the earth and heaven into contact for the redemption of the one by bringing into it the power of the other, " He said, Father," using the word that is to transform humanity as its meaning is understood and accepted. He had come to "show us the Father " and satisfy humanity's

[1] John 16 : 33.

craving. "The hour is come," the crucial hour of creation, the climax hour of His own atoning life, the fateful hour for human destiny, the supreme hour of Infinite Love's manifestation, the hour of sin's ultimate effort and exhibition. "Glorify Thy Son, that the Son may glorify Thee." Glorified suffering, glorified in its purpose, in its bearing, in its influence, so that God the Father shall be glorified. That is the first great idea of the Son's every service.[1]

Verse 2 now defines the method of God's plan and of Jesus' work. God has given Him "authority over all flesh" and in His own person He is to bestow eternal life in actual possession and operation upon a certain definite part of that which is put within His authority. This universal authority along with a quite limited present bestowal of life speaks in accordance with the plans we have already seen presented. The work is to continue and verse 3 defines this eternal life which is to be offered to "all flesh." "This is the life eternal, that they should know Thee, the only true God, and Him whom Thou didst send, Jesus Christ." This is the work that lies before His vision, making known the true nature of God and securing His acceptance through the revealing Christ sent from God. "I made Thee glorious in the earth by finishing the work which Thou gavest Me that I might do it; and now Father I ask that

[1] John 4 : 34; 5 : 30; 6 : 37–38, etc.

Thou wilt glorify Me alongside Thine own self with the glory which I had before the world was by Thy side " (verses 4–5).   Here is a remarkable word if we take it as it most obviously reads in the Greek.   Before the world was the Son was in glory alongside ($\pi\alpha\rho\dot{\alpha}$) the Father.   Then the world came to be alongside ($\pi\alpha\rho\dot{\alpha}$) God also.   But God's glory was not manifest in the earth and so the Son surrendered His glory to glorify the Father in the earth.   This He did by completing an assigned work which was so vital that it is a perpetual work and perpetually increasing.   Now that He has set God's glory in the earth He will desire His own glory restored.   Verses 6–8 state more fully the nature of that work of Christ.   He has manifested the Father's name to the men whom the Father claimed as His own and assigned to Jesus, and they have taken God's word, through Christ, to guard so that God's nature and relation to man can no more be lost on earth. " Now it is matter of knowledge with them that the whole message Thou gavest Me is from Thee, for the words which Thou gavest Me I have given in turn to them and they got them and recognized truly that from Thee I came out, and they believed that it was Thou who didst send Me." [1]   Jesus has set imperishably in human knowledge and life God's nature and message.   This is the seed that will grow into a great tree.   Thus has He laid the

[1] Cf. Ch. 16 : 30 f.

foundation and now on this personal experience of God and His Son He will build His Church and the gates of Hades shall not prevail against it. He has not failed nor been discouraged until He has set true righteousness—God's righteousness—in the earth. Now the isles may wait for Him for in the fullness of the times He will reach them all. The little stone is cut out from the mountain and ready to be set rolling. Here it is, in these illuminated, believing disciples who shall receive power when the Holy Spirit is come upon them.

Jesus has loved His own which are in the world ; He loves them to the limit. He must now pray for them. And as He prays for them standing all around Him they will be impressed anew and indelibly with His deepest longings for them. Hear Him : " I pray in behalf of them." 'Ερωτῶ, I make request that looks for reply. "Not for the world do I pray "—that is not the true order : " Thy way and My way is to move through these believing ones who were Thine—are Thine—and Thou gavest to Me, for Mine and Thine are all the same and in them am I glorified " (verses 9–10). Having found His glory in these believers and looking for its completion in them, Jesus is no longer to be in the world and these are in the world while He returns to the Father ; " Holy Father, guard them in that name of Thine which Thou gavest Me, so that they may be one just as we are. While I was

with them I guarded them in Thy name which
Thou hast given Me and I watched over them
and no one of them was lost but the son of Loss
—and that was in accordance with the Scripture"
(verses 11–12). The name which the Father gave
the Son and in which He has guarded and the
Father will guard believers, what is it? Can it be
other than the name Saviour? [1]

"But now I am coming to Thee and (before
coming) I am saying these things here in the
world in order that they may have the joy that is
Mine perfected in themselves" (verse 13). "I
have given them Thy word and since they thus no
longer are of the world just as I am not of the
world, the world, in which they are, put its hatred
upon them. I request for them, not for them to
be taken literally out of the world (as they are
spiritually taken out of it, for I need them in it),
but that Thou shouldst guard them and keep them
out of the evil. They are not of the world (do not
belong to it and form part of it any more) even as
I am not of the world. Make them holy in the
truth, that is, in Thy word which is the truth"
(verses 15–17). They need to be thus kept,
guarded, unified, sanctified because "As Thou
didst send Me (Thy Son) into the world (to manifest Thy name) so did I, in My turn, send them
(the children whom Thou didst give Me[2]) into the
world"—My mission is projected in them—"and

[1] Cf. Phil. 2:9 f. and Matt. 1:21.   [2] Heb. 2:13.

for their sakes do I devote Myself in order that they also may themselves be devoted truly. Nor do I limit My prayer to these but include also them that believe on Me through their word that all of them may be one " (in spirit, life, work) (verses 19–20).

Now we have come into the third stage of the prayer. Christ's work personally completed is really only begun. It is to be continued and completed in His followers who abiding in the world belong to God and bring God's life ever more and more into the world just as Jesus has set the life of God flowing in mankind. The world for which Jesus will now die, this comes into view in the band of believers growing through the word of these sanctified, believing, witnessing lives. To extend the prayer for them is to bring all the lost world in His heart to the Father. So He prays for all who come to faith through the proclaimed word of this nucleus of faith " that they all may be one in us as Thou Father and I are one " (perfectly at one in all life and plan). And the end of this glorious unity ; " that the world may believe that Thou didst send Me " (verse 21). " Yea on My part I have given to them the glory which Thou hast given to Me—the glory of being one, just as we are one : I in them while Thou art in Me that they may be perfected into one ; and," again let His heart say it, " in order that the world may know that Thou didst send Me and didst love them just as Thou didst love Me." Yea the whole great world must know. Nothing less can satisfy the heart of Jesus the Lord ; and His heart is one with the Father's heart and with the sanctified believer's heart. In this holy aim of world love their glory is to be one (verses 22–23).

Another petition is suggested by the Father's love : " That which Thou hast given Me (a thing already granted and understood between us, but I must bring it forward now) I desire that where I am these too may be with Me (in perfect oneness with Thee and devotion to all Thy thought and will) in order that they may behold the glory that is Mine because Thou hast given it to Me because Thou didst love Me before the foundation of the world " (verse 24). He wants them to understand a love that is eternal before the world was laid down by the hand of the Father-God.

And now in one final burst of passion all His work, all His longing, all His hopes, all His plan find pregnant expression (verses 25–26).

" O righteous Father, the world did not know Thee ; but I knew Thee : (so I came to make the world know) and these came to know that Thou didst send Me ; and I made known unto them Thy (true) name (and character), and will (continue to) make it known ; so that the love wherewith Thou lovedst Me may be in them and I in them." Be it so, dear Lord. Thy heart hath spoken and broken over the world that knew not the Father.

Thou desirest to speak through us of the infinite love of Thy Father—to abide in us.   Be it so, dear Lord.   Guard us still in that name the Father **gave.**

IV

THE MEANING OF MISSIONS TO THE INDIVID-
UAL CHRISTIAN—THEIR AGENT

THAT the responsible agent in the work of missions is the redeemed individual may here be assumed while we inquire what missions mean to him. By virtue of his relation to the Father in heaven, through the Son and Saviour, all that missions mean to God and to Christ Jesus they ought to mean to every man who has experienced the saving power of God's grace in so far as it is possible for the redeemed man, under the influence of God's Holy Spirit, to share the significance of God's great plan in Christ, our Lord. Thus the Bible presents it.

1. It is in the work of missions that the Christian *puts himself in the way of realizing the promises of Jesus :* the promises that are most significant, most necessary, and which Christians are most eager to claim.

(1) It is so of the promises of unlimited answer to prayer. These promises trouble many Christians because they do not seem to be fulfilled in practice. There are several things to be said in answer to such disappointment and perplexity in the face of such apparently limited fulfillment of

unlimited promises that God will give what we ask in the name of Jesus, His Son. The most comprehensive word in reply, and, let us say also, in encouragement, is that these promises, while unlimited, are not unconditioned; perhaps no promise of God to free personality is.

To begin at the beginning we must remember always that we are to ask " in the name of Jesus," and we do well to inquire as exactly as we may what that means.

This name is no conjurer's key for working unnatural and arbitrary results. " Seven sons of one Sceva," " exorcists, took upon them to name over them that had evil spirits the name of the Lord Jesus, saying, I adjure you by Jesus whom Paul preacheth. And the evil spirit said unto them, Jesus I recognize, and Paul I know ; but who are ye ? And the man in whom the evil spirit was leaped on them. . . ." [1]

Similar experience has attended many an effort to name over various matters the name of the Lord Jesus, even where the purpose was less sordid than in this case.

What it is truly to pray in the name of Jesus we may best see by reference to the connections in which the invitations so to pray are given. In the fourteenth chapter of John's Gospel, at verse 10, Jesus emphasizes a teaching He has many times given, that He is perfectly the representative of

[1] Acts 19 : 13 ff.

His Father; "the words that I say unto you I speak not from Myself: but *the Father abiding in Me doeth His works.*" Continuing, He appeals for faith in this unity of Himself and the Father and declares that on such as have this faith devolves the greater part of God's work such as Jesus Himself has been engaged in. Then follows the assurance—it is more than a promise; it is direction for doing the "greater works." "And" —connecting directly with the work to be done (verse 12)—"whatsoever ye shall ask in My name, that I will do in order that the Father may be glorified in His Son. If ye ask Me anything in My name I will do it. If ye love Me, ye will guard the commandments that are Mine, and on My part I will request the Father and He will give you another Paraclete in order that He may be with you forever . . ." (verses 13–16).

Now observe that in Jesus the Father is doing His own work; that those who discern this fact in faith are to do this same Father's work in greater measure; that in doing it they are to ask in the name of Jesus and they can have anything; that the gift of all will come through the coming of the Holy Spirit, taking Jesus' place with the workers; that all this is "in order that the Father may be glorified in the Son." We ask "in the name of Jesus" when standing for Him in God's work we seek the Father's wisdom and power to do what Jesus desires done for the kingdom of God.

Jesus says in phrase most emphatic, as it appears in the Greek, " If ye love Me, the commandments that are Mine will ye guard, and I, on My part, then will request the Father " (verses 15–16).

Again in chapter fifteen, pointing out the relation between Himself and His disciples, that the purpose of this union is much fruit bearing, Jesus again promises (verse 7): " If ye abide in Me and My words abide in you, whatsoever ye desire ask and it shall come for you." But we must not stop with this, for Jesus goes right on : " In this was My Father glorified (" was " having reference to the Divine plan) in that ye bear much fruit and ye shall be to Me disciples " (verse 8). Continuing His appeal and explanation He says again (verses 15–16): " No longer do I call you slaves, for the slave knows not what his lord does : but I have called you friends because all things that I heard from My Father I made known to you. Ye did not choose Me but I chose you and appointed you in order that you might go away and bear fruit and that your fruit might remain ; (all this idea of your work being, again [1]) in order that whatever you may ask the Father in My name He may give you." Clearly the Father may not make such gift unless those praying are following the course of " friends " to whom the plan of God has been made known by Christ. Later Jesus tells the

[1] In the Greek there is a new purpose clause for this prayer statement.

sorrowing disciples that He will see them again and fill them with permanent joy, after His resurrection, of course, He means ; and that from that time they will no longer come to Him, as now and heretofore, but in His name will go to the Father and "If ye shall ask anything of the Father, He will give it you in My name." [1]

It was doubtless in memory of the teaching of Jesus on this occasion that John was led to write long afterwards : "Beloved, if our heart condemn us not, we have boldness towards God ; and whatsoever we ask we receive of Him, because we are keeping His commandments and doing the things that are pleasing in His sight." [2]

To James it was given to teach that prayer goes unanswered because it is selfish "that ye may consume it on your own desires." [3]

Jesus teaches us to pray first of all for the Father's glory and kingdom to come perfectly on earth, while for ourselves we seek only the necessary things. [4] Not all the prayer promises are, in their connection, related to this kingdom work, to be sure. Yet it is evident enough that this is the most emphasized condition. Add one word more of the Master : "Verily I say unto you, What things soever ye shall bind on earth shall be bound in heaven ; and what things soever ye shall loose on earth shall be loosed in heaven. Again I say

---

[1] John 16 : 23.   [2] 1 John 3 : 21–22 ; cf. 1 John 5 : 14–15.
[3] James 4 : 3.   [4] Matt. 6 : 9–12.

unto you (and in face of such responsibility a further word is necessary) that if two of you shall agree on earth as touching anything that they shall ask it will come to them from the presence of My Father who is in heaven. For where two or three are gathered together in My name, there am I in the midst of them." [1]

(2) So also of the promise of Christ to be present in the life of the Christian. The Scripture just quoted assures the presence of the Lord where two or three are gathered together *in His name*, and the whole promise is for the work of " binding" and "loosing" on earth for heaven's confirmation. This is not merely implied in the Upper Room teaching already studied ; [2] it is explicitly set forth. Whenever, and in the measure, that the disciples are one with the Father and the Son the world will come to know the Father. That is the immediate end of this unity. It is in connection still with "the greater works" to be done by His followers that Jesus says, "I will come unto you. Yet a little while and the world will see Me no more, but ye see Me, because I live, and ye shall live. In that day ye shall know that I am in My Father and ye in Me, and I in you. He that hath My commandments, and keepeth them, it is he that loveth Me ; and he that loveth Me shall be loved of My Father. I, too, will love him and will make Myself evident to him.   If a man love Me,

[1] Matt. 18 : 18–20.   [2] Chap. III.

he will guard My word, and My Father will love him and we will come unto him and will make our abode with him." [1]

Most familiar, perhaps, and most cherished of all the forms of this promise is the " Lo, I am with you all the days even unto the end of the world." It is impossible legitimately to dissociate this promise from the command universally and fully to evangelize the nations. It is only when engaged in this task that we may claim or realize this promise. Its very form, when rightly rendered, emphasizes this ; " all the days even unto the consummation of the age "—the completing of the Gospel age is the objective of the promise.

(3) The promise to supply even material needs is made only to those who are seeking God's kingdom and righteousness so primarily and persistently as to have become careless of food and raiment. " After all these things the heathen seek " but followers of Christ are to be seeking the heathen for Christ.[2] All these *things* may be —are—given to many others, they are promised unfailingly to the servants of Christ who are carrying His Gospel to men.

Christ was careful to teach His disciples that it is to those who " for His sake and the Gospel's " suffer loss of goods and friends that a hundredfold shall be given here in this life.[3]

[1] John 14 : 18-23.   [2] Matt. 6 : 31-33.
[3] Matt. 19 : 28 ; Luke 18 : 29 f.

(4)   The gift of the Holy Spirit is bound up in the same important condition. " Ye are witnesses of these things.   And behold I send the promise of My Father upon you " are the words in which Jesus gives the promise in Luke 24 : 48 f.   Exactly the same relation is recorded in John 20 : 21 f., " As the Father sent Me even so send I you.   And when He had said this He breathed on them and said, Receive ye the Holy Spirit, whosesoever sins ye forgive they are forgiven   .   .   .   " ; and also in Acts 1 : 8, " Ye shall receive power when the Holy Spirit is come upon you and ye shall be My witnesses both in Jerusalem and in all Judæa and in Samaria and unto the uttermost parts of the earth."

We have seen how the prayer promises and presence promises of John 14–16, are bound up inseparably with the world witness work committed to the " friends " of the Christ.   Of course this includes the Holy Spirit promises also.   The world has seen and hated Jesus and the Father. " But when the Paraclete is come whom I will send unto you from the Father, the Spirit of Truth who proceedeth from the Father, He shall bear witness of Me ; and ye, too, bear witness.   .   .   ." [1] " It is advantageous for you that I go away, for if I go not away the Paraclete will not come unto you ; but if I go I will send Him unto you ; and He, on coming, will convict the world.   .   .   ." [2]   Subjec-

[1] John 15 : 23–27.   [2] John 16 : 7 f.

tively considered, for these few disciples alone, it might not be better to exchange Jesus for the Paraclete.   But so soon as we understand that they are sent into the world to " convict the world " with reference to sin, righteousness and judgment, we can see readily enough why they should " exchange the presence of Jesus for His omnipresence," His help for His " power."   The conditions of the promise correspond exactly to the history of fulfillment as recorded in the Acts and expounded in the Epistles.

2.   To the Christian man *missions are his means of carrying to fellow men the highest possible good.*

All that the Christian message means, in itself and its consequences, the missionary carries to the man in pagan darkness and papal servitude.

Some one has said that it is the privilege of the Christian to go to this man and that and give to him God.   By such service the follower of Christ becomes, secondarily, a giver, an originator, a creator, a redeemer, and all in the spiritual sphere where his work is eternal.   " Make all the nations learners from Me—enter them in My school ;— baptizing them into the new relation and possibilties implied by the names Father, Son, Holy Spirit ; then leading them on to guard the whole teaching of Him who taught you." [1]   Such is the commission of the missionary.   Or as it appears in Paul's commission : "   .   .   .   the heathen

[1] Cf. Matt. 28 : 19 f.

unto whom I send thee to open their eyes that they may turn from darkness to light and from the power of Satan unto God, that they may receive remission of sins and an inheritance among them that are sanctified in Me"; [1] a form of expression which was still in Paul's heart when years afterwards he writes to the Colossians [2] of "giving thanks unto the Father who made us meet to be partakers of the inheritance of the saints in light; who rescued us out of the power of the dark and brought us over into the kingdom of the Son of His love." Such is the gift of missions in all ages. We give expression to "the tender mercy of our God whereby the dayspring from on high shall visit us, to shine upon them that sit in darkness and the shadow of death." [3]

In the fifteenth chapter of Romans Paul outlines his own missionary principles from the standpoint of the appeal of heathen need in a way that may well be taken as the model for all.

Writing to a church composed of Jewish and heathen elements, each inclined to judge the other, the Apostle makes a great plea for fraternal helpfulness (chs. 14–15), and concludes the appeal, "Wherefore receive ye one another, even as Christ also received you, unto the glory of God" (verse 7). He then proceeds to enforce this idea of receiving "for God's glory" by presenting his

---

[1] Acts 26 : 17 f. [2] Col. 1 : 12.
[3] Luke 1 : 78 f. ; cf. Isa. 9 : 1 ff. ; 60 : 1–3.

conception of Christ's function and the place Paul himself holds in it, supporting his position by four quotations from the Old Testament. Read his argument (verses 8–24): "For I say that Messiah has come to be a minister of the circumcision (Israel) in behalf of God's truth, with a view to fulfilling faithfully the promises made to the fathers and—this further function with reference to the heathen—that they may glorify God, too, for His mercy." To Jews the Messiah is the expression of God's truth, to heathen of God's mercy, to all the means of God's glory. And this is exactly in accord with God's revealed purpose, as it is written:

"Therefore will I confess Thee among the heathen,
And sing to Thy name." [1]

And again it says,

" Rejoice, ye heathen, along with His people." [2]

And again,

" Praise the Lord, all ye heathen ;
And let all the peoples praise Him." [3]

And again, Isaiah saith, [4]

" There shall be the root of Jesse,
And He that ariseth to rule over the heathen,
On Him shall the heathen hope."

" Now," continues Paul, " may the God who held out this hope to the heathen and who Himself hopes for their redemption, [5] fill you with all joy

[1] From Ps. 18:49.   [2] From Deut. 32:43.   [3] From Ps. 117:1.
[4] Isa. 11:10.   [5] " The God of hope," objective and subjective.

and peace in believing so that ye may overflow in hope in the power of the Holy Spirit "—that by sharing God's feeling about the heathen you may hope for the salvation of the heathen by means of the Holy Spirit's power, and may have joy and peace in believing in this larger hope of God's Gospel. " I am persuaded, my brethren, even I myself—the Gentile missionary—concerning you that you are yourselves, too, full of goodness, filled with all knowledge (as to this plan of God) able also to admonish one another (in cases of failure to apprehend).   But I write the more boldly to you briefly, as reminding you because of the (special) grace given to me from our God with a view to my being Christ Jesus' messenger unto the heathen, as their priest [1] ministering God's good news so that the heathen's offering might come to be acceptable, being sanctified in the Holy Spirit. I have therefore for my glorying in Christ Jesus the things pertaining to God.   For I will not dare in any respect to speak of things which Christ did not accomplish through me for the obedience of the heathen (working through me) by word and deed in the power of signs and wonders, in the power of the Holy Spirit (making it unquestionable that God was claiming these heathen), so that from Jerusalem and round about even unto Illyricum I have fulfilled the (preaching of) good news of the Messiah, being ambitious to proclaim the

[1] ἱερουργοῦντα.

good news not where Christ was called by name (but where He was unknown) so that I might build not upon the foundation of another but (might be fulfilling that prophecy) just as it is written,[1]

" They shall see to whom no tidings of Him came, and they who have not heard, shall understand. Wherefore I was hindered these many years from coming unto you: (He could not come while in his way lay heathen who had not heard the good news): but now, having no more any place in these regions, and having these many years a longing to come unto you whenever I may go into Spain—for I hope in passing through to look upon you and by you to be brought on my way thither if with you I shall first be partially filled." Such is the great Apostle's yearning for men in the darkness and distress of heathenism. Finding warrant in God's Word he must unceasingly labor to bring to them the good news of the Messiah and bring them to the God of hope who waits to receive them with the Holy Spirit's proofs of approval. To this service of bringing the heathen to God Paul, and every other true missionary, devotes his life and feels that " even if I am poured out as a drink offering upon the sacrifice and service of your faith, I rejoice and rejoice with you all " and calls on these heathen thus so blessed in coming to God to " rejoice and rejoice with me." [2]

[1] In Isa. 52: 15.   [2] Phil. 2: 17.

The appeal of them that are " without God and without hope in the world " is irresistible to the man whom the love of Christ constrains ; " because we thus judge, that one died for all, then they all died (and so are in death now) ; and He died in behalf of all in order that they who (have been made to) live may no longer live for themselves, but for the One who died and rose again in behalf of them "—all them for whom He died—all men. [1]

3. *In missions we become workers together with God in fulfilling His promises to Christ and in all that the work of missions means to Him.* God's electing grace determines the times and the seasons [2] while the missionary " endures all things for the elect's sake that they may attain to the salvation that is in Christ Jesus with everlasting glory." [3]

So the early workers thought of themselves. When Peter and John had been before the Sanhedrin for preaching Jesus on " being let go, they came to their own company and reported all that the chief priests had said unto them."   Then all prayed together, recognizing that this is in accordance with God's Word and that God's hand is in it all.   "And now Lord," they make petition, " look upon their threatenings ; and grant unto Thy servants "—not immunity from suffering ; that matters not, but--" with all courage to speak

[1] 2 Cor. 5 : 14 f.   [2] Eph. 1 : 10 ; Acts 1 : 7.   [3] 2 Tim. 2 : 10.

Thy word, while on Thy part Thou stretchest forth Thy hand to heal; and that signs and wonders may come to pass through the name of Thy holy Servant Jesus." Two things they desire, courage and coöperation from God. " And when they had prayed, the place was shaken wherein they were gathered together; and they were all filled with the Holy Spirit, and they spoke the word of God with courage."[1] The coöperation was complete.

When controversy arose over the terms on which the missionaries were admitting heathen converts to Christian fellowship and the subject was under discussion at Jerusalem, Paul and Barnabas appealed to the proofs that they were working in coöperation with God, " And all the multitude kept silence ; and they hearkened unto Barnabas and Paul, rehearsing what signs and wonders God had wrought among the heathen through them." The argument was final, " And after they held their peace, James answered" with the proposal which was unanimously adopted as that which "seemed good to the Holy Spirit and to us."[2] While not a part of the genuine text of Mark, the final verse of the sixteenth chapter tells how the matter was regarded in the first age of the Gospel ; " And they went forth and preached everywhere, the Lord working with them, and confirming the Word by the signs that followed."

[1] Acts 4: 23-31.   [2] See Acts 15 : 12 ff., 28.

Jesus had entrusted His Gospel witness to the Holy Spirit and to His followers. [1]

In 1 Corinthians 3 : 9, Paul says "we are God's fellow workers" and he amplifies this thought in 2 Corinthians 5 : 20–6 : 2. Having shown that Christ died for all, that those made alive in Christ are for His service in the interest of those yet dead ; that God has committed unto us the ministry—the actual work—of reconciliation of the world unto Himself through Christ, the Apostle declares :   "We are ambassadors therefore on behalf of Christ as if God were calling (men) on through us :   We beg, (men, generally, not ' *you*,' it is a statement of the ambassadors' function) Be ye reconciled to God."   "God was in Christ reconciling the world unto Himself." Christ, not visible and recognizable in Himself to the world, is in us and so it is that "in Christ's behalf we are God's ambassadors to men."   Christ's function is seen in that, " Him who knew no sin He made to be sin in our behalf that we might become God's righteousness in Him."   (In Christ we become the expression, the declaration of God's righteousness to men, seems to be Paul's thought here.   The idea is not theological but practical, missionary, as Paul sets it forth.)   "And (now that we have thus been brought into this responsible position) working together we too entreat that you do not receive the grace of God in vain.   For He

[1] John 15 : 26 f.

saith:[1] At an acceptable time I hearkened unto
thee, and in a day of salvation did I succor thee ;
behold, now is the acceptable time ; behold now
is the day of salvation." Now is the time for
faithful beseeching on the part of the ambassadors.

4. *By means of missions we allow Jesus to carry
forward His self-realization in us.*   It is thus that
we further the work, to completion, that our Lord
began ; carry on in our bodies what is lacking of
the afflictions of Christ for His body's sake ; justify His confidence in us in undertaking such a
work reckoning on our service ; prepare for His
return in glory to reign ; satisfy the dear desire of
His heart.

We now examine some of the Scriptures thus
summarized.

It is with reference to continuing his work that
Paul gives expression to the " earnest expectation
and hope that in nothing shall I be put to shame
but with all courage as always so now also Christ
shall be magnified in my body, whether by life or
by death."[2]   A bold thought, but realizable for
every servant of Christ by the supply of the Spirit
of Jesus Christ: making larger the Christ for the
vision of men.   Men are so far from Him that
His splendor and grace do not appear for salvation until they pass through the magnifying lens
of consecrated lives, bringing the Saviour near
the needs of ignorant and sinful men.   Paul has

[1] In Isa. 49 : 8.   [2] Phil. 1 : 20.

another bold, good word on this subject in Colossians 1 : 24–29 : " Now I rejoice in my sufferings in behalf of you and I am filling up on my part that which is lacking of the afflictions of the Messiah in my body for the sake of His body, which is the Church, of which (Church) I became a minister according to the stewardship of God which was given to me for you to fulfill God's word (about saving the nations), the secret that has been hidden from the ages and from the generations but now was manifested to His saints to whom God was pleased to make known what is the wealth among the heathen of the glory of this secret, which (rich secret) is God in you (Jews and heathen alike) the hope of glory : " a work to which the Apostle is wholly devoted " striving according to the energy of Christ which is energizing in me in power." Christ's energy is displaying mightily in the missionary Apostle the rich grace of God now seen to include the nations. By the sufferings in His own person Christ Jesus redeemed His Church ; by His afflictions in the bodies of His servants does Christ gather that Church from all the ends of the earth.

That they were witnesses of the things of Christ [1] the first disciples understood and affirmed repeatedly,[2] and they realized that it was through them that Jesus would be able to project Himself

[1] See Luke 24 : 48; Acts 1 : 8.
[2] Cf. Acts 2 : 32; 3 : 15; 5 : 32; 13 : 31.

outward and onward among men and accomplish
that for which He was come into the world, the
greater part of which so far as its application was
concerned must ever appear in the work of believing men.[1] It was only after such universal
testimony that Jesus would come again to earth in
glory,[2] and for this coming followers of Jesus must
look and hasten.[3] For this consummation our
Lord waits, while also, in His saints, He powerfully works ; waits through the centuries, waits in
confidence until His witnesses do their work for
Him. Wonderful indeed is it to think how, trust-
ing in the promise of Jehovah, Jesus could lay
down His life in a work whose success depends so
largely on the fidelity of redeemed humanity.

"Jehovah said unto My Lord, Sit Thou at My
right hand,
　Until I make Thine enemies Thy footstool.
　Jehovah will stretch forth the sceptre of Thy
strength out of Zion :
　Rule Thou in the midst of Thine enemies.
　Thy people offer themselves willingly
　In the day of Thy power in holy array ;
　Out of the womb of the morning
　Thy youth are unto Thee as the dew."

Thus in Psalm 110 do we see the picture which
has its growing fulfillment in every age when
missions flourish. We may see the New Testament counterpart of this Old Testament vision in

[1] John 14 : 12.　　　[2] Matt. 24 : 14.　　　[3] 2 Peter 3 : 12

Hebrews 10 : 10–13.   The spirit of Messiah is expressed in the words " Lo I am come to do Thy
will " (verse 9).   " In which will (of God which
was the law of the life of Jesus) we have been set
apart (to carry it out along with Jesus) through
the offering of the body of Jesus Christ once for
all " (it remaining only to apply that " offering "
through our Gospel).   In contrast with the daily
offering of the priest " which can never take away
sins," " He, when He had offered one sacrifice for
sins, for all time took His seat at the right hand
of His God,[1] as for the rest awaiting in expectancy
until His enemies are placed as the footstool of
His feet."   There He sits to-day awaiting the fulfillment of the work of His servants, and at the
same time working with them in the abundant
power of His Spirit.

5.   It is a summary inference from all this significance of missions to say now that here *the Christian
finds the best possible investment for his life ;* in
partnership with God, in coöperation with the
Holy Spirit, in the greatest possible service to men,
accomplishing the greatest work of the ages and
bringing to pass the completed will of our Christ.

Facing death within two days and facing at the
moment some inquiring heathen Greeks, our Lord
says, " The hour is come that the Son of Man
should be glorified."   Facing death a little ahead
and inquiring heathenism all around, the time has

[1] Cf. now Ps. 110: 1.

come when every saved son of man should be
glorified.   Jesus lays down the principle for us all:
" Verily, verily, I say unto you, Except a grain of
wheat fall into the earth and die it abideth by itself alone; but if it die it beareth much fruit.   He
that loveth his natural life loseth it; and he that
hateth his natural life in this world shall guard it
unto eternal life.   If any man serve Me let him
follow Me (and we should know now where He
leads, in the darkness of earth's rebellion and
need) and where I am (now am, not shall be in
glory) there also the servant that is Mine will be:
if any man serve Me My Father will honor him"
(John 12 : 20–26).

V

THE MEANING OF MISSIONS TO THE CHURCH
—THEIR CONSERVATOR

" CHRIST loved the Church and gave Himself up for it ; that He might sanctify it, having cleansed it by the washing of water, in a word, that He might set the Church at His side, glorious, not having spot or wrinkle or any of such things, but that it might be holy and blameless." [1]   The Church constituted for Christ an entity, unifying in one conception all His redeemed on which He lavishes an infinite love, in which He sets His glory and upon which He sets His hopes.   This Church He will set by His own side ; and we find Christ and His Church set thus together in the Scripture.   Christ is Himself the Saviour of the Church as His body and nourisheth and cherisheth it ; [2] or, under His own figure, builds it on the foundation of personal experience of Himself as the Son of God.[3]   It will be best for us to study this Church in two aspects as related to missions.

I.   *The Church General : i. e.,* the spiritual body of the redeemed, apart from tangible organization, since no organization is coëxtensive with the

[1] Eph. 5 : 25–27.   [2] Eph. 5 : 23, 29.   [3] Matt. 16 : 16–18.

105

Church.   As such the Church is *first* the exposition to the universe of God's wonderful wisdom and glory ; and *second* the realization of Christ's body in its completeness, and of His love in the world.   Thus there are relations to God, the Father of our Lord Jesus Christ and so the Church's Father ; and to the Redeemer Lord whose bride the Church is.

(1)   In the first chapter of Ephesians [1] Paul gives a remarkable outline of the Christian call in its logical stages and relations : (1) in the loving foreordination of the Father, choosing us in Christ (verses 3–6); (2) in the gracious historical redemption in the blood of the Saviour (verses 7–13 a) ; (3) in the pledging sealing of the Holy Spirit (verses 13 b–14).

At the end of each one of these sections, which together compass the entire scheme, scope and plan of redemption, the Apostle is careful to insist : that the entire work is " according to the pleasure of God's will for the praise of the glory of His grace wherein He was gracious to us in the Beloved " (verse 6) ; that the unfolding of the plan was wise and prudent, regarding " the fullness of the times," still " in accordance with the purpose of Him who worketh all things according to the counsel of His will, to the end that we should be unto the praise of His glory " (verse 12) ; that the

[1] Remember that this is a general letter to several churches in the province of Asia.

final complete redemption of God's own sealed possession is to be " unto the praise of His glory " (verse 14).

So in chapter three the Apostle tells how the secret plan of redemption's progress has now been revealed wherein the " bringing to the nations the good tidings of the unsearchable riches of the Messiah and the making all men see how God has disposed the ages " looks to the end " that now unto principalities and powers in the heavenlies might be made known through the Church the many-sided [1] wisdom of God " (verses 8–11).[2]

With such a function it is small wonder that no part of the Church, no age of its history shall be made perfect apart from the whole, God having provided some better thing for us.[3]

Seeing such a relation of the Church to the eternal God we may well ponder deeply the prayer to which the Apostle calls us when he has outlined the redemption call of our God.   Find it in Ephesians 1 : 15 ff.   " On this account I, too, on hearing of the faith in the Lord Jesus that is with you, and of the love which includes all God's holy ones (His Church, then) do not cease giving thanks in your behalf, making mention in my prayers that the

---

[1] Literally " many-colored," hence showing itself only partially at a given moment and requiring time for its full understanding and appreciation.

[2] Cf. Chap. II where this entire passage is discussed.

[3] Heb. 11 : 40.

God of our Lord Jesus Christ, the Father of glory,
may give you a spirit of wisdom and revelation in
the accurate knowledge[1] of Him (Christ), the eyes
of your hearts having been opened to the end that
you may know (three things), (1) What is the hope
of His calling (*i. e.*, what God looked forward to
in calling you, the praise of the glory of His grace
so emphasized in the argument that leads up to
this prayer), (2) What is the riches of the glory of
God's inheritance in His saints (what comes to
God Himself when the redeemed are set apart for
Him in Christ Jesus), (3) What is the abounding
magnitude of God's power (coming) into us who
have faith, even in accordance with the energy of
the might of His strength which He showed in the
Messiah when He raised Him from the dead and
set Him down at His own right hand in the
heavenlies up beyond every rule and authority
and power and lordship and every name that is
called not only in this age but also in the coming
age." Such is God's relation to, and estimate of,
His Church which He wishes us to understand.

"Now to Him that is able to establish you according to my Gospel and the heralding of Jesus
Christ, in accordance with the revelation of a secret hidden for age-times but now both manifested
by means of prophetic Scriptures and, according
to the commandment of the God of the ages, made
known unto all the nations with a view to their

[1] ἐπιγνώσει.

obedience of faith: to the only, wise God (His wisdom manifest) through Jesus Christ, to whom be the glory forever, Amen " (Rom. 16 : 25–27).[1] As the Church makes known her Lord does she reveal the wisdom and effect the glory of God in the universe.

(2)   In the account of his prayer for his readers in the first chapter of Ephesians Paul came to speak of the exaltation of Jesus by His Father: he then adds, " And all things He arranged in subjection under His (the Son's) feet, and Him He gave as head over all things to the Church which is His body, the fullness of Him who fills all things in all respects." [2]   The Church is the fullness—the full expression—of Christ who contains in Himself all God's redemptive plan and work.   Not only does this belong to the passage here which has just told how God exalted Him; but in Colossians 1 : 19 and 2 : 9 we are told how it was pleasing that in Christ should " dwell bodily all the fullness of God."   There is no redemptive act or movement of God that the Scriptures do not locate as in Christ, just as there is no movement of man in redemption that is at all available apart from Jesus.   He is emphatically, for God and for man, the Redeemer.   What limitless contents must be crowded into this conception of the Church, the body of Christ, as herself in turn the fullness of

[1] Cf. 11 : 33–36; Phil. 4 :20; 1 Tim. 1 : 17; 1 Pet. 4 : 11; Jude 24–25; Rev. 1 : 6.   [2] Verses 22–23.

Him that in all respects fills all.   We do not need here to consider the Gnostic error which has influenced, by its negation, the form of Paul's expression, for, entirely apart from that, we have here a clear statement of a transcendent truth.[1]

In Ephesians 4 : 8–16 we find the practical statement of the principle, first given in its abstract, general form in the passages just now under consideration.   With chapter four we reach the turn in the argument.   Up to this point there is an exposition of the call of God ; from this point there is an appeal that we shall live worthily of the calling wherewith we are called, with instructions for this worthy walk.   First of all is a plea for unity in the Church (verses 3–6), along with the recognition of individual responsibility for the personal gift to each one from Christ (verse 7).   Then the gifts to the Church and their purpose are presented : " Wherefore He saith : When He ascended on high He led captive a band of captives, and distributed gifts unto men. . . .   He that descended is the same also that ascended far above the heavens that (in this position of authority and power) He might fill all things (carrying to full completion His work of redeeming and subjecting all things to God)."   His band of captives was just those men whom the Father had given Jesus out of the world and whom He had bound inseparably to Himself, for

[1] Cf. in this connection John 1 : 1–3.

His service. These He now distributes, in His
wisdom, to men. " And He gave some as apostles, and some as prophets, and some as evangelists, and some as pastors and teachers (pastor-
teachers), for the purpose of perfecting the saints
for the work of service to the end of building up
the body of the Messiah until (to the extent that)
we all (all that go to make up that body) come fully
into the unity of the faith and the accurate knowledge of the Son of God (and so come also) into
full manhood, unto the standard of the stature of
the fullness of the Messiah "—until the Messiah's
wish and work are fully accomplished in the
Church. And now, indicating the growth needed
(verse 14) the end is further indicated with a slight
change of figure : " but being true in love may in
all respects grow into Him who is the Head,
Christ, from whom all the body, fitly framed and
knit together, through every joint of the supply
(given by the ascended Christ) according to the
working in due measure of each separate part
makes increase of the body to the building up of
itself, in love." All these classes of ministers
are given with a view to perfecting the private
saints in service so that the body of Christ may
come to full and complete maturity—until the
Perfect Head shall have a complete body with all
its elements, every part, in place and perfect.
Here is the concrete application, for human service, of " the plan of the ages laid down in Christ

Jesus," unfolded in the first part of chapter three. In view of such an ideal we must summon ourselves to join Paul's prayer and doxology in the latter part of that chapter.[1] Remember that the prayer was about to begin at 3 : 1, when the Apostle turned aside to explain the scope of the redemption scheme in order that we might say to the prayer an amen intelligently in sympathy with its great ideals. Hear now the prayer : " For this cause (because God is in Jesus Christ making a new humanity of the broken race and you have been called into it) I bow my knees unto the Father, from whom all idea of fatherhood and family, in heaven and on earth is derived (and so who is rightly to be recognized as Father by all men—to whom all ought to come in obedient sonship); that He would grant you, in accordance with the wealth of His glory, [2] powerfully to be strengthened by means of His Spirit (coming into and energizing) into the inner man (the result of this being the further gift) : that the Messiah shall dwell through faith in your hearts, you being rooted and founded (both figures are necessary at all to carry the great thought) in love, to the end that you, along with all the saints (it is needful that they all come to this height of sympathetic understanding) may be strong enough to comprehend [3] what is the breadth and length and height and depth and (in a word), to know the knowl-

[1] Eph. 3 : 14 ff.   [2] Cf. 1 : 6, 12, 14.   [3] Literally, *to get down*.

edge-surpassing love of the Messiah, in order, finally, that you may be filled up to all the fullness of our God."

When we take into account the relation of this prayer to the entire epistle, its specific connection with the explanation of the redemption secret of God, in this chapter; and the meaning which Paul always puts into the term "fullness," we cannot understand the prayer, as is generally done, to refer primarily to God's love for ourselves and to our coming into the full glory of God. No, the Apostle seeks in the saints a dwelling-place for *the Messiah*—and he has not used the article (ὁ Χριστὸς) carelessly here—a dwelling-place for the Messiah in the true humanity made strong by faith and the indwelling Spirit, so that in us the Messiah can go on with His redeeming work. We must, to this end, understand the broad reach of the Messiah's love to all men in all lands; its long reach to all men from the first age to the last; its depth reaching to the gates of death and hell; its height lifting to the bosom of the Father —a four-dimension love that truly goes beyond human knowledge. The Church must come to contain and express in itself all the fullness of God in redemption—must indeed be the fullness of Him who in all respects fills all things. Is such knowledge too deep for us? Is it so high that we cannot attain unto it? Hear the Apostle again, speaking by the Holy Spirit: " Now to the

One who is beyond all things able to do abundantly more than we ask or think—and to do it on
the basis of the power that is already working in
us, to Him be the glory in the Church and in
Christ Jesus (God's glory in the two united) unto
the generations of the age of the ages." Are we
ready now to join in Paul's "Amen"?

2. We must now think of *the Church organic ;*
the smaller concrete body through which the spiritual body expresses itself and, so to say, becomes
conscious of itself. In this smaller, tangible, concrete body chiefly does the Church exercise its
functions and discharge its obligations.

To, and of, such a body Paul wrote in 1 Corinthians 12–14, of the relations of the members of
the body, calling upon all to recognize the same
Spirit, the same Lord, the same God in all their
gifts. "For as the body is one and hath many
members, and all the members of the body, being
many, are yet one body ; so also is Christ."[1]

"Now ye are the body of Christ and members
of it each in his part."[2]

In such a local organization Paul finds that God
"hath set various gifts, beginning with missionaries."[3] The term can hardly mean technically
Apostles in this connection, while missionaries
renders it exactly.[4]

To this church the Apostle says : "Awake to

---

[1] 1 Cor. 12: 12.
[3] 1 Cor. 12: 28.
[2] 1 Cor. 12: 27.
[4] See Chap. IX.

soberness and sin not ; for some have no knowledge of God ; I speak to move you to shame," [1]
and it is a shame to any such **church,** when its sin
has left any ignorant of God.

Now all the words concerning the Church general we have been studying will find the channel
for their practical acceptance and application in the
concrete organization we now have before us.
One may note especially how the passage, with
the most concrete illustration of all, in Ephesians
4 : 3–16, can be best realized in concrete organisms,
and it is significant that while there it is said generally that the ascended Lord "gave gifts unto
men" of various ministers, in 1 Corinthians 12 : 28
it is said that God hath set in the church (local
and specific) various ministers.   The ultimate aim
is the same, the perfecting of the body of Christ
in service for its complete life in Him.

The most immediate duty of the concrete small
body in missions is to deepen and perfect the work
of grace intensively, and fully to evangelize its
own locality.   The standpoint from which the
New Testament presents the relation of this church
to missions leads us to speak rather of what the
church is to missions than of what missions mean
to the church.   Missions are first, the organized
church is afterward.   The kingdom of heaven is
the great end of believing prayer and labor.   One
frequently meets the question, "What is the place

[1] 1 Cor. 15 : 34.

of missions in the Church?" The right question is, "What is the place of my church in missions?" Our Lord talked constantly of the kingdom; on only two occasions did He speak of the Church and on one of these occasions He uses it in the general sense as equivalent to the kingdom of heaven in its temporal relation—the body of redeemed in time. [1]

How then do we find the church so prominent in the thought of the followers of Christ when they had entered upon the discharge of His commission? In answer it will be well to note first the exact facts. The Gospels and Acts are, of course, general historical works, though Luke and the Acts are directed, perhaps, to an individual, but with a universal aim. Of Paul's epistles, Romans, Ephesians, Colossians, are addressed to "the saints" in definite locations; 1 and 2 Corinthians, 1 and 2 Thessalonians to definite "churches" in their organized capacity; Galatians to "the churches in Galatia"; Philippians to "the saints in Christ Jesus that are at Philippi with the pastors and deacons"; 1 Timothy and Titus officially to ministers and 2 Timothy semi-officially also; Philemon is a wholly personal letter to one of the missionary's converts and helpers concerning another convert and helper. The Epistles of James, Peter, Jude and 1 John are general, 2 John to a church (probably) 3 John to an individual to com-

[1] Matt. 16: 16 ff.

mend his heroic stand in support of missionaries. Hebrews is an appeal to Jewish Christians, a class that had speedily come into a relation of dependence upon the larger freedom of spirit and material possession of Gentile believers.   The Revelation is addressed " to the seven churches that are in Asia." Now all these churches had grown up under the labors of the missionaries and to conserve and continue the work begun by the first heralds of the Gospel.   The identity and dignity of these churches seems to be carefully guarded and Apostolic care is bestowed on each one.   In the small province of Asia each city must have its own church and each church its own special " Angel " through whom comes a message peculiarly adapted to that organization from Him who walketh in the midst of the golden lamp-stands holding their stars in His right hand.[1] He who thus guards the separate church in its locality is the same who " made us for a kingdom, priests unto God even His Father "[2] and "for whom men shall pray continually "[3] that " to Him shall be the glory and the dominion forever and ever." [4]

For that other province of Galatia Paul writes not to one but to several churches.[5]   In every place where converts were made the Apostles were careful to organize them into a coöperative body and to "appoint them elders in every church,"

---

[1] Cf. Rev. 1–3.   [2] Rev. 1 : 6.   [3] Ps. 72 : 15.
[4] Rev. 1 : 6.   [5] Gal. 1 : 2.

encouraging them with helpful instruction on **their** entering into the kingdom of God,[1] while later on they will return and visit the brethren in every city where they had proclaimed the word of the Lord to see how they fared.[2] How these churches shared in "the furtherance of the Gospel" beyond their own territory we shall have occasion to consider elsewhere.

But while the Lord's missionaries are devoting so much care to the founding and care of churches it is apparent enough that they have not lost sight of the ideal of the kingdom of their Lord. That fills still the horizon of their hopes and is the goal of their toil and sacrifice. In the church they have found the effective working organization of the kingdom. There can be little doubt that the constitution and function of this institution are included in the "all things" of the Master's teaching.[3] They were of the Lord's founding who acquired each one with His own blood, and were erected by the Holy Spirit, who appointed overseers for the flock[4] and "he that hath an ear" must heed "what the Spirit saith to the churches."[5] Every such institution whose existence is justifiable came to be and continues for the purpose of extending, deepening, perfecting the kingdom. It is not primary but secondary, not an end but a

---

[1] See Acts 14 : 22 f.   [2] Acts 15 : 36.
[3] Cf. Matt. 18 : 15–20.   [4] Acts 20 : 28.
[5] Rev. 2 : 7, and at close of each of the seven messages.

means, not existing for itself but for the kingdom, hence not eternal but temporary. Between the everlasting kingdom and the eternal spirit the church serves a function of helping the one in entering and extending the other. It combines, enlarges, inspires, restrains and conserves the work of individuals who are devoting themselves for the Lord's sake and the Gospel's in seeking the kingdom. They train and fit for service,[1] and become bases for further extension.[2] Such being the function of the church in the kingdom we may readily sum up the meaning of missions to this unique institution :

(1) The reason for its existence—causal and final reason. The church is the product of missions and exists to promote them. One does not forget the nurture of Christian character in the members but this nurture is " for the work of service."

(2) " The law of the life of the Church " for Warneck's words [3] will apply to the church local as well as to the Church general.

(3) The supreme proof of loyalty to the Lord— a test which applies first to the individual Christian and through him to the church. The church is a lampstand and when it no longer serves to illumine the darkness the lampstand is removed out of its place.

---

[1] Eph. 4 : 11 ff.   [2] Cf. 1 Thess. 1 : 8.
[3] " Outline of the History of Protestant Missions."

(4) A channel and conservator for other bless-ings in the church.

(*a*) It tends to promote harmony among all the churches and more than anything else conduces to that unity of spirit and faith in the whole Church, which was so earnest a desire of the Master and care of the Holy Spirit.

(*b*) It tends to doctrinal purity. Of churches as of individuals it is true that willingness to do the Lord's will brings power to discern between true and false teaching.[1]

(*c*) Brings preparation and inspiration for all the life and work of the church. The educational and inspirational "value of a great idea" is be-yond compute. The idea of bringing in the king-dom of heaven for the redemption of men and the glory of God, once it becomes the formative prin-ciple of a life or of an organization, has brought with it the power of the Infinite.

History quite justifies this Scriptural conclusion.

[1] John 7 : 17.

VI

THE MEANING OF MISSIONS TO THE WORLD
—THEIR BENEFICIARY

THE world of men is the object with which God and redeemed men are engaged. What, then, do missions signify to the world? We must not forget ourselves here. We are making a Bible study and must not deal with the meaning of missions, in a more general way, for the world's commerce, science, education, culture, all forms of human progress—a most fascinating study and the most unanswerable Christian apologetic.[1] The Bible teaches the religious significance of Christian missions for the world.

1. Missions bring *the fulfillment of all right religious ideas and aspirations.* The missionary meets the men who are seeking God with the object of their search. Before every altar to " the unknown God," in temple or on hilltop, in heart or on hearthstone, the missionary is able to proclaim to the worshippers: " What ye worship in

[1] Cf. "Christian Missions and Social Progress," Dennis; "Christianity and the Progress of Man," Mackenzie; "The Great Commission," Harris; "Missions and Culture," Warneck; "Gesta Christæ," Brace, etc.

ignorance, this I set forth for you; the God that made the world and all things in it. . . ." [1]

Every man whose heart is jealous for his God cannot but have "his spirit convulsed within him," like Paul at Athens, when he sees the idolatry of his fellow men. This discerning man sees also in this idolatry a ground of appeal with hope of success. Such men are clearly religious and where religion is, Christianity may be; and it must be if man's religions are to reach their legitimate goal.

One of the mightiest appeals to the missionary spirit of the Gospel is the religiousness of humanity. All men are conscious of religious need; of dependence on, and obligation to, somewhat more and higher than themselves and with which they would fain have fellowship. These needs and longings find expression in the ethnic religions. This is the attitude of the Bible towards honest religion in heathen men. That gross immorality, sordid and licentious self-indulgence in the name of worship is condemned and punished by the God of the Bible is no refutation of our position. Pharisaism in the name of Jewish religion called forth the most unsparing condemnation from our Master but this involved no censure of their law or the prophets, every word of which He would honor in their fulfillment. Missions here rest on the principle so grudgingly accepted and so slowly

[1] Acts 17 : 23 f.

adopted by Peter and some other early disciples :
" Of a truth I perceive that God is not a respecter
of persons, but in every nation he that feareth Him
and worketh righteousness is acceptable to Him."[1]

The quick logic of slow reason may conclude :
" Then there is no need for missions."   Not so the
righteous mind taught by the redeeming love of
God's Spirit.   This is the Spirit that bade Peter
go with the messengers of Cornelius " making no
distinction," and the same that caused Cornelius
to see " the angel standing in his house, and saying, Send to Joppa, and fetch Simon, whose surname is Peter, who shall speak unto thee words
whereby thou shalt be saved, thou and all thy
house."   The same Spirit also it was who, as
Peter began to speak, " fell on them as on us at
the beginning." [2]   The conclusion of the whole
matter was that " to the heathen God hath granted
repentance unto life." [3]

Cornelius was "a devout man and one that feared
God with all his house, who gave much alms to
the people, and prayed to God always," and his
prayers and alms went up for a memorial before
God.[4]   God's response is not to accept him as he
is, requiring and doing nothing further.   God's
way is to send to Cornelius a missionary of
the Gospel to speak unto him words whereby he
shall be saved, and others are to be saved by the

[1] Acts 10 : 34 f.   [2] Acts 11 : 9–15.   [3] Acts 11 : 18.
[4] Acts 10 : 1–4.   See following verses for further reference.

same words.   Then God manifests approval in the miracle of the Holy Spirit.

When Barnabas and Paul find their miracle of healing the cripple at Lystra rewarded with the ignorant worship of the natives they are horrified, to be sure, but answer sanely : " Gentlemen, why do ye these things ?   We also are men of like passions with you, and bring you good tidings, that ye should turn from these vain things unto a living God, who made the heaven and the earth and the sea, and all that in them is : who in the generations gone by suffered all the heathen to walk in their own ways.   And yet He left not Himself without a witness, in that He did good and gave you from heaven rains and fruitful seasons, filling your hearts with food and gladness." [1]   The spirit of worship is not at all condemned but is used as a basis for the good news of the living God.   So great is the sense of superstitious worship that the missionaries could scarce restrain the multitudes from doing sacrifice unto them, [2] an experience with many a parallel in modern mission work.

The Word of God clearly recognizes the religious faculty and its groping for light and truth. Not all the blind are without the capacity to have their eyes opened and many that are deaf to the uncertain voices of Nature and natural insight will gladly hear the joyful sound of the good message of the Saviour.   " Bring forth the blind people

[1] Acts 14 : 15-17.   [2] Verse 18.

that have eyes, and the deaf that have ears. Let all the nations be gathered together and let the peoples be assembled : who among them can declare this and show us former things ? " Challenge the history of all the religions of the peoples, and their present condition. Compare them honestly with the message of our Christ. " Let them bring their witnesses, that they may be justified, or let them hear, and say, It is truth. Ye are My witnesses, saith Jehovah, and My servant whom I have chosen, in order that ye may know and believe Me, and understand that I am He : before Me there was no God formed, neither shall there be after Me. I, even I, am Jehovah ; and besides Me there is no Saviour. I have declared, and I have saved and I have showed and it is no new thing among you : [1] therefore ye are My witnesses, saith Jehovah, and I am God." [2]   Such is God's challenge and He depends on His witnesses to convince the devotees of all other religions that they may listen and accept the truth. When " the love of Christ constrains us " this challenge takes on the full missionary spirit and we find ourselves " the ministers of Christ Jesus unto the heathen ministering in sacrifice the good news of God

---

[1] The translators indicate by italics that the reading " there was no strange *God* among you " is an interpretation, not a translation. We submit our rendering to the judgment of the reader. It seems to fit exactly the connection and is as faithful to the original as the other.

[2] Isa. 43: 8–12.

so that the offering of the heathen may be made acceptable by being sanctified by the Holy Spirit." [1] To teach the heathen how to do acceptably what they blunderingly fail at is one aspect of the mission opportunity. Is it not the mission of the Messiah "to guide our feet into the way of peace"? [2]

Be it so that "the ethnic faiths" are the best answers the religious spirit of man can make to the questions of man's soul. Christianity is God's answer in Christ Jesus. He speaks in the missionary.

2. *Missions bring to men of all the world deliverance from religious ignorance, superstition and oppression.* "The times of this ignorance God overlooked but now commandeth men that they should all everywhere repent," [3] and He overlooked that He might spare them until the fullness of the times when the Gospel should make manifest the savor of God's knowledge in every place, [4] even "in all creation under heaven." [5]

If the religion of humanity constitutes an impelling appeal to the Christian to give God's true message, so, too, does man's irreligion and perversion of religion appeal pathetically for restraint, correction and guidance. The ignorance of true principles of religion and of all else that speaks distinctly of God and of the destiny of the soul; the superstitious fears and hopes that hold in ap-

---

[1] See Rom. 15 : 16.   Luke 1 : 79.   [3] Acts 17 : 27.
[4] 2 Cor. 2 : 14.   [5] Col. 1 : 23.

palling bondage so many millions of the race of men ; the bondage of spirit to slavish fears and the bondage of life to priests of ignorance and superstition who prey upon the ignorant dread and blind hope of helpless religious feeling ; these appeal with powerful pathos to all who, knowing the Light, will stop to look upon the condition of them that are in darkness.

The clear vision of the Evangelical Prophet who saw the coming Servant on whom Jehovah would put His Spirit [1] beheld that Servant with a mission to all God's world : " Thus saith God Jehovah, He that created the heavens and stretched them forth ; He that spread abroad the earth and that which cometh out of it ; He that giveth breath unto the people upon it, and spirit to them that walk therein : " asserting His provident care and love claim on all men as a basis of His commission to His Servant : " I Jehovah have called Thee in righteousness and will hold Thy hand and form Thee (shape Thy career) and give Thee for a covenant of the people, for a light of the nations ; to open the blind eyes, to bring out the prisoners from the dungeon, and them that sit in darkness out of the prison house." That Jesus regarded this as spoken of His mission in the world He has Himself made clear.[2]   That there is

[1] Isa. 42 : 5 ff.
[2] Cf. specifically Luke 4 : 18 ff. where Jesus applies to Himself the similar passage from Isaiah 61.

direct reference to heathen religious corruption is part of the word we read here : " I am Jehovah, that is My name ; and My glory will I not give to another, neither My praise unto graven images " (verse 8) ; and the effect of such practices on the standing of the heathen worshippers is also announced : " They shall be turned back, they shall be utterly put to shame, that trust in graven images, that say unto molten images, Ye are our gods " (verse 17). Jehovah has fulfilled His word in the past and is now announcing new things before they spring forth (verse 9). There is then a prophetic call to all : " Sing unto Jehovah a new song, and His praise from the end of the earth ; ye that go down to the sea, and all that is therein, the isles and their inhabitants " (verse 10). Places heretofore destitute of religious knowledge are to give glory and praise to Jehovah's name for He is now going forth to do mightily against His enemies (verses 11–13). For a long while the heathen have been left to develop their folly and helplessness but this shall be so no longer. Jehovah has " held His peace, been still, refrained Himself," but now will call strenuously against such a state of degraded religion (verse 14) and will use natural powers to rebuke such ignorance (verse 15) ; " And I will bring the blind by a way that they know not ; in paths that they know not will I lead them ; I will make darkness light before them, and crooked places straight. These things will I do and I will not abandon them " (verse 16). An invitation is urged on the deaf and blind to see and hear (verse 18). The pity of it all is that the people who should be Jehovah's servant and messenger to these in darkness and ignorance are themselves blind and deaf (verses 19–22) ; and a call must be made for some to " give ear, hearken and hear for the time to come " that the way of Jehovah may be explained to men so that they may understand how His displeasure is expressed against religious perversions and degradations (verses 23–25).

Again, in Isaiah 44, Jehovah calls, as the Only God, King and Redeemer, for some to stand in His place and for Him call to men and declare His past dealings and future plans with men. Those who offer for this service have no cause to fear or be afraid.[1] " Have I not declared unto thee of old, and showed it ? and ye are My witnesses. Is there a God besides Me ? Yea there is no Rock ; I know not any " (verses 6–8). The need and the hope of such a mission is seen in the utter folly of image-making and the utter ignorance of the priests of idolatry—" their witnesses see not, nor know " (verses 9–11). The strenuous zeal and care with which a man employs himself and others to make him a god out of a

---

[1] Cf. John 14 : 27 where Jesus uses almost exactly this language to His missionaries whom He is sending out for just the work portrayed in Isaiah.

tree, other parts of which are used for ordinary functions is a pathetic picture (verses 12-17). "They know not, neither do they consider ; for one hath daubed their eyes, that they cannot see; and their hearts, that they cannot understand. And none calleth to mind, neither is there knowledge nor understanding to say, 'I have burned part of it (the tree) in the fire (for warming my body) ; yea, also I have baked bread upon the coals thereof ; I have roasted flesh and eaten it ; and shall I make the residue thereof an abomination ? Shall I fall down to the stock of a tree ?' He is feeding on ashes ; a deceived heart hath led him astray ; and he cannot deliver his soul, nor say, ' Is there not a lie in my right hand?'" (verses 18-20). Surely a sad, true picture of the state of a religious spirit in religious bondage. And the next paragraph is an exhortation for God's people, formed to be His servant, to remember these things, "for Jehovah hath redeemed Jacob" from such bondage "and will glorify Himself in Israel."

Missions bring to these "prisoners of hope" the power to open their eyes that they may turn from darkness to light and from the power of Satan unto God, that they may receive remission of sins and an inheritance among them that are sanctified by faith in Him who died "that He might deliver them who through fear of death were all their lifetime subject to bondage." [1]

[1] Acts 26 : 18 and Heb. 2 : 15.

3. Another aspect of the blessing of *missions* to the world is that therein is *the world's opportunity to know God*. It is by this means they are delivered from the bondage of blind religions and realize the true end of the religious impulses implanted forever in the nature of man's spirit.

It is at this point that the insufficiency of all non-Christian religions becomes most evident. The deepest cry of the human spirit is its call for God. Of the three fundamental elements of religion, dependence, obligation and fellowship, the peculiarity, the glory of Christianity, is in the sphere of fellowship. Other religions stress dependence and issue in fatalism, or emphasize obligation and enslave the masses to guilty fears administered by oppressive priests. Not one of them brings man face to face with a God who, remaining Himself high and holy, yet knoweth our frame, remembereth that we are dust, and who, like as a father pitieth his children, pitieth them that fear Him ; whose eye is upon His children for guidance and His ear open to their cry. Moses in the beginning had challenged Israel ; " For what great nation is there that hath a god so nigh unto them as Jehovah our God is whensoever we call upon Him?" [1] Abraham, the father of believers in our God, was the " Friend of God " and all who come into His fellowship Jesus calls " no longer servants but friends." " Truly our fellowship

[1] Deut. 4 : 7.

is with the Father and with His Son Jesus Christ." [1]

Now contrast with this the best ethnic religions. Confucianism knows only an impersonal heaven and can offer the soul no hope for fellowship with even the highest finite spirits ; Buddhism bids the soul seek as its highest good absolute indifference in a Nirvana freed from experiences; Hinduism has no holy personalities and its goal is the loss of one's own personality in the indefinite Brahma ; Mohammedanism offers not even communion with the prophet who is himself far down below the highest heaven of Allah's presence.

Our Lord's deepest lament for men is that they do not know His righteous Father,[2] and the highest good, eternal life, consists in coming to know the Father as the only true God and Jesus Christ as the one sent by the Father.[3]

The great sin of hating, rejecting, opposing Jesus, was that men were thereby missing and repudiating His Father,[4] and the consummation of discipleship to Jesus was the getting to be at one with the Father.[5]

This meaning of the Gospel to heathen men, the first of missionaries has summed up for us in Ephesians 2 : 11–22. He contrasts the condition before the Gospel comes with that into which

[1] I John I : 3.   [2] John 17 : 25.   [3] John 17 : 3.
[4] Cf. John 15 : 23 f., and many similar passages.
[5] John 17 : 22, etc.

the heathen are led under the good message:
"Wherefore keep in mind that once ye, the
heathen, in flesh, those called Uncircumcision by
that which is called Circumcision (it is only) in the
flesh (and) handmade (not at all of the essence or
touching the spirit where religion is ; keep in mind
then) that at that time ye were without a Messiah
(since ye were in a condition) alienated from the
commonwealth of Israel and outsiders of the covenants of the promise (of redemption in God's Messiah) ; not having a hope and Godless in the
world.[1]

"But now (in glorious contrast) in Christ Jesus,
ye, the (very) ones then far off, came to be near in
the Messiah's blood.   For He (Himself emphatically) is our peace, the One that made the two
(races) one, having broken the wall of division,[2]
enmity, in His flesh having nullified (rendered inoperative) the law of commandments in dogmas
(merely dogmatic injunctions) in order that the
two He might in Himself create into one new humanity by making peace and so might restore the
two, in one body, reconciled to God by means of
His cross, having in it slain enmity.   And (in accordance with this view) having come He told the
good news of peace to you, the ones far off, and

[1] The word is $K\acute{o}\sigma\mu o\varsigma$.

[2] Literally "the wall of the fragment " or "of the breaking": an
artificial wall that temporarily divided what in God's counsels is essentially one and all under His love.

peace to those near. Because through Him we
have our access, both of us, in one Spirit unto the
Father. Take notice,[1] therefore, no longer are ye
outsiders and men not at home (in the worship of
God)[2] but rather are ye fellow citizens of the
saints, members of the household of our God,
having been built upon the foundation of the
Apostles and prophets, Christ Jesus Himself being the chief corner-stone; in whom every building, fitly framed together (with the rest), grows
into a temple, holy in the Lord, in whom you too
are being built in into a dwelling-place of our God
in the Spirit." Such is the changed relation to
God offered to the races of men in missions.

4. *Missions mean the world's chance to know
Jesus Christ.* All turns on that. If Jesus were
only man and still such a Master as we find Him,
the world needs above all others to know Him.
When Jesus is God our Saviour, humanity's need
of Him is infinite and imperative. We have said
that religions are tested by their offer of fellowship
with God and that herein is Christianity unique.
This fellowship is the gift of Christ. "Neither
doth any know the Father save the Son, and He
to whomsoever the Son willeth to reveal Him."[3]
But the Son's announced aim is the fulfillment of
the prophecy, "And they shall all be taught of
God."[4]

---

[1] The uniform meaning of the particle ἄρα.   [2] Cf. Isa. 56 : 3 ff.
[3] Matt. 11 : 27.   [4] John 6 : 45 ; cf. Isa. 54 : 13; Jer. 31 : 34.

If Jesus "is the propitiation for the whole world," we, when "we have beheld," "bear witness that the Father hath sent the Son *to be* the Saviour of the world."[1]   "There is no distinction between Jew and Greek; for the same *Lord* is Lord of all and is rich unto all that call upon Him; for, Whosoever shall call upon the name of the Lord shall be saved.[2]   How then shall they call on Him in whom they have not believed? and how shall they believe in Him whom they have not heard? and how shall they hear without a preacher? and how shall they preach except they be sent?   .   .   . So belief cometh by hearing and hearing by the word of Christ." This argument, which Paul[3] supposes may be made against his contention of salvation by faith in Jesus, is admitted by him as valid, and he held that "by the word of Christ," all are to have "the hearing."

Paul again exhorts that "supplications, prayers, intercessions, thanksgivings be made for all men." "This is good and acceptable in the sight of God our Saviour; who desires all men to be saved and to come into full knowledge of the truth.   For there is (but) one God, one mediator also between God and men, Himself a man Christ Jesus, the one that gave Himself a ransom in behalf of all, the testimony *to be borne* in its own times, unto which testimony I was appointed a herald, and an

[1] I John 4: 14.   [2] Cf. Joel 2: 32.
[3] In Rom. 10: 12–17.

Apostle (I speak the truth, I am not lying), a teacher of heathen in faith and truth." [1]

There is but one God and He wishes all men to be saved and to be fully instructed. This can be only if they know Jesus Christ who is the one Mediator bringing men and God together. This Mediator gave Himself as a ransom in behalf of all. The testimony of this ransom is to be borne at the time suited for it. That time has now come. The proof is that Paul himself holds appointment for just this service, to teach heathen men faith and truth. On such a basis rests his call for all his churches to interest themselves in all men.

"We turn to the heathen" because "so hath the Lord commanded us: I have set thee for a light of the Gentiles, that thou shouldst be for salvation unto the uttermost parts of the earth." [2]   And as it was in the days of this first missionary journey so it is still; "On hearing this, the heathen are glad and glorify the Word of God ; and as many as are ordained unto eternal life believe." [3]

5.   It is involved in all we have been saying, from the Word of God, that *missions mean for the world the only hope of salvation*.   This truth is contained in each phase of meaning already studied and is declared in many Scriptures.

If the words of the Psalmist [4] are true of this

[1] 1 Tim. 2: 1-7.   [2] Acts 13: 46-47, quoting Isa. 49: 6.
[3] Verse 48.   [4] Ps. 49: 7-9.

present life all the more do they apply to the life eternal :

" None can by any means redeem his brother
Nor give to God a ransom for him
That he should still live alway
That he should not see corruption,
For the redemption of their life is costly
And must be let alone forever." [1]

Human help is powerless in redemption, which is within the power of the name of Jesus Christ, crucified and raised from the dead : " And in none other is there salvation ; for neither is there any other name under heaven, that is given among men, wherein we must be saved." [2]

With another application Paul has written words that summarize the attitude of God's Word on this subject : " We know that no idol is *anything* in the world, and that there is no God but one.   For there be that are called gods, whether in heaven or on earth ; as (in actual fact) there are gods many, and lords many ; yet to us there is one God, the Father, of whom are all things and we unto Him ; and one Lord Jesus Christ, through whom are all things, and we through Him.   Howbeit there is not in all men that knowledge.   .   ." [3] In Romans 10 Paul insists that this limitation of salvation, as through the Christ, applies even be-

---

[1] For the sake of clearness the order of verses 8, 9 is reversed ; cf. any version.

[2] Acts 4 : 12.   [3] I Cor. 8 : 4-7.

fore the Incarnation, and, as we saw above, accepts the reasoning that men cannot be saved without the ministering of the Gospel of Jesus Christ. We saw also above the emphatic insistence upon the sole mediatorship of Jesus between God and men [1] which must be duly witnessed to all men.

Through Isaiah we read Jehovah's declaration [2] " Assemble yourselves and come ; draw near together ye that are escaped of the nations : they have no knowledge that carry the wood of their graven image, and pray unto a god that cannot save.   Declare ye and bring it forth ; yea let them take counsel together (to make the best possible showing for heathen worship) ; who hath showed this from ancient time ? who hath declared it of old ? have not I, Jehovah ? and there is no God else besides Me, a just God and a Saviour ; there is none besides Me.   Look unto Me, and be ye saved, all the ends of the earth ; for I am God, and there is none else.   By Myself have I sworn, the word is gone forth out of My mouth *in* righteousness and shall not return, that unto Me every knee shall bow, every tongue shall swear.   Only in Jehovah, it is said of Me, is righteousness and strength ; even to Him shall men come ; and all they that were incensed against Him shall be put to shame.   In Jehovah shall all the seed of Israel be justified, and shall glory."   " Seed of Israel " can here be understood only in the Gospel sense.

[1] I Tim. 2: 5–7.   [2] Isa. 45 : 20–25.

This position of God's Word, so fully read in its pages, has been decried as exclusiveness. Such a charge forgets God's reason for this position. "If a law had been given which could make alive, verily righteousness would have been of law. But the Scripture shut up all things under sin, in order that the promise by faith in Jesus Christ might be given to them that believe"; [1] and "God hath shut up all unto disobedience, that He might have mercy upon all." [2]

Jesus gave the keys of the kingdom to His followers because only by this Gospel key is it possible for any to enter in. He gave the key for admitting and not for excluding as the Roman Church seems to hold and as overzealous Protestant dogmatists are too apt to suppose. All God's effort looks to bringing men into the kingdom of the Son of His love. Instead of questioning the righteousness of excluding men from His kingdom unless they enter by the door of the Redeemer all who love their fellow men will the rather join with God in seeking and saving the lost.

"Deliver them that are carried away unto death

And those that are tottering to the slaughter see that thou hold back.

If thou sayest, Behold we knew not this;

Doth not He that weigheth the hearts consider it?

[1] Gal. 3: 21 f.

[2] Rom. 11 : 32.

And He that keepeth thy soul, doth not **He** know it?

And shall not He render to every man according to his work?"[1]

That all that has been adduced in this chapter has its application to Roman Catholic lands and people should be obvious enough; and the appeal of these should come into the hearts of all who would see zealous religionists find "the accurate knowledge of the Son of God";[2] who would see the worship of God freed from the ignorance of formalism, the superstition of baptized heathenism, the bondage of priestcraft and ecclesiasticism; who would that all believers might "have their access through Christ, by one Spirit unto the Father"[3] and "come boldly unto the throne of grace that they may receive mercy and may find grace to help in time of need";[4] whose ambition is that men may know Christ Jesus our Lord and the power of His resurrection; who pray "that all men shall be saved and come into clear knowledge of the truth."[5]

[1] Prov. 24 : 11-12.   [2] Cf. Eph. 4 : 13.   [3] Eph. 2 : 18.
[4] Heb. 4 : 16.   [5] 1 Tim. 2 : 4.

VII

THE MISSIONARY MESSAGE

WE have now to study somewhat more specifically the message with which missions come to men.

1. First let us undertake to state the *content of the message*. It is a message of salvation to sinners, a message of reconciliation to rebels, a message of light, life, love to men in spiritual darkness, death, despair. Such a message must be framed with the utmost skill powerfully to persuade the rebellion, clearly to illumine the ignorance, and justly to remove the sin and guilt of them that have gone away from God so that

"All the ends of the earth shall remember and turn unto Jehovah;

And all the kindreds of the nations shall worship before Him (Thee)." [1]

All these conditions are met in the person and work of the Christ incarnate "who was delivered up for our trespasses and raised for our justification." [2]

(1) It is to the risen Lord Himself that we go for the first unfolding of the message He will send to men. In "the Great Commission" on the day

[1] Ps. 22 : 27.

[2] Rom. 4 : 25.

141

of Ascension the chief emphasis is laid on the duty
and responsibility of the followers to go with the
message.   The content of the message is not then
given, according to the record of Acts 1 : 6–10.
So also when the Lord met the " above five hundred " on " the mountain where Jesus had appointed them in Galilee " the record [1] does not
contain the content of the message : rather we
read that Jesus is sending them, with His absolute
authority in heaven and on earth, to make of all
the nations learners of Him, pledging these new
pupils in the Teacher's school by the badge of
baptism in the name of the Triune God, then
teaching them to carry out in life all the Teacher's
lessons ; finally pledging His own continuous
presence with the messenger.

For the summary of the message itself we come
to the first lesson of the Lord, alive from the dead,
with His timid disciples.   We find the record in
John [2] and, more complete, in Luke.[3]   John's account : " When therefore it was evening on that
day, the first of the week, and when the doors
were shut where the disciples were, for fear of the
Jews, Jesus came and stood in the midst, and saith
unto them, Peace unto you ; " beginning where
He had left off with them three nights ago.   But
how much has come to pass since then !   They
are slow to believe or to comprehend.   " And
when He had said this He showed unto them His

[1] Matt. 28 : 16–20.   [2] John 20 : 19–23.   [3] Luke 24 : 36–49.

hands and His side," at once the proofs of His identity, the ground of this " peace " He so insists upon, the pledge of eternal love that makes peace and secures it. " The disciples therefore were glad when they saw the Lord " and it is to be theirs to make very many glad by causing them to see the same Lord, with the scars in His hands and feet and side and with the word of peace in His mouth. " Jesus therefore (because joyous appreciation of Him is taking the place of gloomy doubts and fears) said to them again (now to emphasize and extend indefinitely in their minds His words), Peace unto you : as the Father hath sent Me, even so send I you." How the Father had sent Him He has been telling them these three years, but the sum of it is now made up in the peace, based on His sufferings, which they must take to men. " And when He had said this He breathed on them, and saith unto them, Receive ye the Holy Spirit (thus symbolically bestowed as soon actually to come for their work of proclaiming peace to men): whosesoever sins ye forgive, they are forgiven unto them ; whosesoever ye retain they are retained." He will now rely wholly on His disciples, with the Holy Spirit upon them.

Luke has the same facts but much more fully recounted. Not only does He show them His hands and His feet after the first message of " Peace unto you," but argues from these proofs of identity, and then eats before them to prove further that He is no mere spirit.[1]   And now having brought them to a calmer joy and peace in His presence He proceeds to make them understand Him as never before : " And He said unto them, These are My words which I spake unto you while I was yet with you, that all things must needs be fulfilled, which are written in the law of Moses, and in the prophets, and in the Psalms, concerning Me.   Then opened He their mind that they might understand the Scriptures. "[2]   We must at this point pause and seek to reconstruct the picture Luke intends to suggest to us.

It will help us here to recall the walk of the two to Emmaus[3] to whom, as they were excitedly discussing the strange reports and rumors of resurrection, Jesus appeared, unknown, and chided them with foolish slowness of heart, for " Was it not needful for the Messiah to experience these things and to enter into His glory ?   And beginning from Moses and from all the prophets He interpreted to them in all the Scriptures the things concerning Himself."   When at their home " their eyes were opened and they knew Him ; and He vanished out of their sight," they recalled how " their hearts were burning within them while

[1] See verses 36–43.

[2] Is not this, in part, Luke's equivalent for John's saying that " He breathed on them and said, Receive ye the Holy Spirit " ?

[3] See verses 13–35.

Jesus opened to them the Scriptures." "And they rose up that very hour, and returned to Jerusalem, and found the eleven gathered together, and them that were with them. . . . And they rehearsed the things *that happened* in the way, and how He was known of them in the breaking of the bread." It was upon this rehearsal that Jesus came into the upper room. The two had been telling of the Scriptures the Lord interpreted for them when the Interpreter comes to take up His own task. They now stand around Him in peaceful joy and amazed wonder as He takes now this roll, and now that, and goes over with them the things concerning Himself, first in the Law of Moses; then in the Prophets; then in the Psalms. How their hearts now burned within them and how the hours of that eventful night ran away as He led them from roll to roll of the Holy Scriptures, from Messianic word to Messianic word, opening up, in the Resurrection's light and the Spirit's illumination, the wonderful scheme of Redemption in which He was the Redeemer of men! How many sections of the Old Testament He opened up to them and just which we cannot know. One may feel quite safe in suggesting that among them were such as these: (*a*) "In the law of Moses": Genesis 12 : 1–4, the first comprehensive outline of the Messianic plan; Exodus 19: 5–6, the function of the Messianic race; Deuteronomy 10 : 12–19, the right attitude of the Messianic people

towards others; and from the laws of sacrifice in
Exodus and Leviticus the Messianic types; (*b*)
"And in the prophets" such passages as Joel
2:28–32; Micah 4:1–5; 5:2–5; Isaiah 7:14;
9:1–9; 11:1–10; 19:18–25; 40:3–5; 42:1–9;
43:1–13; 44:1–5; 49:1–26; 51:4–6; 52:13–
53:12; 59:15–60:14; Zephaniah 3:8–10; Jeremiah 16:19–21; Ezekiel 39:21–22; Daniel 2:44–
45; 7:13–14, 27; Zechariah 2:9–13; (*c*) "And
in the Psalms" these are obvious, 2, 22, 50, 67,
72, 80, 98, 110.

We remind ourselves again that we cannot be
sure of all these passages, but in many of them we
can have no question that we are following the
words Jesus interpreted to His followers in the upper room on that first Lord's Day evening and
night.

At length He leaves off the interpretation and
turning His eyes upon their souls He said, "That
is how it stands written;" as to the two of Emmaus
earlier He had said, in effect, "That is the way it
must be." Thus it is written, and thus it ought
to be written, for so is the will of the eternal
Father. He alone who reads his Bible thus finds
in that Bible what God put there in the interpretation of His Son. Jesus then proceeds to sum up
the teaching, giving us the message and naming
the messengers.

First: "The Messiah must suffer, and rise again
the third day;" this is, according to God's re-

vealed will and plan, and according to the history, the basis for the salvation of all men.

Second: "That repentance and remission of sins should be preached in His name;" here is the universal and necessary condition of that salvation through the Messiah.

Third: "Should be preached in His name unto all the nations, beginning from Jerusalem;" there is need that this salvation and its condition be universally preached.

Fourth: "Beginning from Jerusalem, ye are witnesses of these things;" they who know Jesus are to begin where they are to proclaim their witness until the message is carried to all the nations.

Fifth: "And behold I send forth the promise of My Father upon you; but tarry ye in the city, until ye be clothed with power from on high." The power to make the message effective is of the Holy Spirit; the witnesses are to wait for Him, but expecting Him, they must wait even where they are.

(2) If now we turn to the message delivered by the first missionaries, we find that they follow exactly the lines laid down by the Master. Peter was the Apostle to the Jews and Paul to the Gentiles and it is of these two we find distinct account of their message.

Of Peter we have account of five occasions when he delivered the missionary message. The first is

on Pentecost.[1]   Having explained the cause of
the remarkable conduct of the disciples he proceeds to his message : " Ye men of Israel, hear
these words :   Jesus of Nazareth, a man approved
of God unto you by mighty works and wonders
and signs which God did by Him in the midst of
you, even as ye yourselves know ; Him being delivered up by the determinate counsel and fore-
knowledge of God, ye by the hand of lawless men
did crucify and slay ; whom God raised up, having loosed the pangs of death because it was not
possible that He should be holden of it."[2]

Enforcing this fact from the Old Testament Scriptures, he declares : " Let all the house of Israel
therefore know assuredly, that God hath made
Him both Lord and Christ, this Jesus whom ye
crucified " (verse 36).   Then the people having
cried out in conviction, the preacher tells them
what to do :   " Repent ye and be baptized every
one of you upon the name of Jesus Christ unto the
remission of your sins ; and ye shall receive the
gift of the Holy Spirit."[3]   He proceeds to enforce
this duty and then the three thousand are taken
into the fellowship of the Lord's followers.

Here we find just the points Jesus expounded
for them on the Resurrection evening :   The suffering of Jesus and His resurrection ; declaring
Him to be the Messiah of God; on account of which
men must repent and have their sins removed.

[1] Acts 2.   [2] Verses 22–24.   [3] Verse 38.

To the crowd that thronged Peter and John and the man to whom they had just brought healing[1] Peter explains : " The God of Abraham, and of Isaac, and of Jacob, the God of our fathers, hath glorified His Servant Jesus, whom ye delivered up and denied . . . whom God raised from the dead ; of which we are witnesses. . . . But the things which God foreshowed by the mouth of all the prophets, that His Messiah should suffer, He thus fulfilled. Repent ye therefore, and turn again, that your sins may be blotted out. . . ."[2] The same message with the emphasis on just the same points and the outcome is that " many of them that heard the word believed."[3]

Before the Sanhedrin, too, instead of a defense we find the declarations :[4] " Be it known unto you and to all the people of Israel, that in the name of Jesus Christ of Nazareth, whom ye crucified, whom God raised from the dead, even in Him doth this man stand here before you whole ; " and, then, " We cannot but speak the things which we saw and heard." The death and resurrection of God's Messiah, bringing salvation, and we the witnesses.

In the same way Peter presents his testimony a second time before the Sanhedrin.[5] " The God of our fathers raised up Jesus whom ye slew, hanging Him on a tree. Him did God exalt at His

[1] Acts 3.   [2] Verses 13-19.   [3] Acts 4 : 4.
[4] Acts 4 : 10-20.   [5] Acts 5 : 29-32.

right hand as Prince and Saviour, to give repentance to Israel and remission of sins.   And we are
witnesses of these things, and the Holy Spirit,
whom God hath given to them that obey Him."

Finally, before Cornelius and the company of
his family and friends, we hear this Apostle again
delivering the same message.[1]   "The word which
He sent unto the children of Israel, preaching
good tidings of peace by Jesus Christ (He is Lord
of all) . . .   whom also they slew, hanging
Him on a tree.   Him God raised up the third day
and gave Him to be made manifest . . .   unto
witnesses that were chosen before of God, to us
who ate and drank with Him after He rose from
the dead.   And He charged us to preach unto the
people and to bear witness that this is He who is
ordained of God *to be* the Judge of the living and
the dead.   To Him bear all the prophets witness,
that through His name every one that believeth
on Him shall receive remission of sins."   Here,
when for the first time the good news is being
delivered to Gentile (heathen) men, Peter seems to
be taking especial pains to follow out exactly the
lines laid down by Jesus in the passage we have
studied.   And it cannot have escaped us that the
Holy Spirit has His recognized part on every one
of these occasions.   It would be interesting to
study Peter's epistles in this connection, especially
their dedications.   But we must forbear.

[1] Acts 10 : 34-43

Come now to Paul, who stands alongside Peter
as an Apostle-missionary.   He is more independent in thought and expression than Peter.   He has
come into his knowledge of the Messianic Redeemer in a manner wholly different from Peter
but it is to the same Lord, from whom also he has
got the same message for the world, as any one
can see who will compare the message to the
eleven in Luke with that to Paul in Acts 26.

To the Corinthians he sums up his Gospel
(1 Cor. 15 : 1–11) : "Now I make known unto you,
brethren, the good tidings which I preached unto
you. . . .   For I delivered unto you first of all
that which also I received ; that Christ died for our
sins according to the Scriptures ; and that He was
buried ; and that He hath been raised on the third
day according to the Scriptures ; and that He appeared. . . ."   Or, as he expresses it in
Romans 4 : 24 f, where he speaks of " us . . .
who believe on Him that raised Jesus our Lord
from the dead, who was delivered up for our trespasses, and was raised for our justification."

The human response to God's appeal in the
risen Messiah required by the Gospel Paul sets
forth in his address to the elders of the church at
Ephesus,[2] " testifying both to Jews and to Greeks
repentance towards God and faith towards our
Lord Jesus Christ."

If we would hear Paul delivering this message

[1] 1 Cor. 15 : 1–11.   [2] Acts 20 : 21.

to the heathen we have only to turn to the account
of his work in Antioch in Pisidia.[1]   Here, perhaps
because of the initial character of this work in the
missionary preaching, we have a full outline of
Paul's sermon.[2]   He shows God's progress in the
history of grace leading up to the time when
"God according to promise brought unto Israel a
Saviour, Jesus."

Then he tells how the Scriptures were fulfilled
by the rejecting Jews : " And when they had fulfilled all things that were written of Him, they
took Him down from the tree, and laid Him in a
tomb.   But God raised Him from the dead ; and
He was seen for many days of them . . . who
are now His witnesses unto the people."   Then
after showing the conformity of these facts with
the Scriptures he makes application :   " Be it
known unto you therefore, brethren, that through
this man is proclaimed unto you remission of
sins ; and by Him every one that believeth is
justified from all things. . . ."

Later at Thessalonica " where was a synagogue
of the Jews," " Paul, as his custom was, went in
unto them, and for three Sabbath days reasoned
with them from the Scriptures, opening and
alleging that it behooved the Christ to suffer, and
to rise again from the dead, and that this Jesus
    .   is the Messiah." [3]

So we find Paul, just as the rest, making the

[1] Acts 13 : 16 ff.   [2] Verses 16–41.   [3] Acts 17 : 1–3.

main points of his missionary message just the points emphasized in the Master's instruction. The Scriptures show that the Messiah must suffer and die and be raised from the dead ; Jesus has fulfilled these conditions and is just such an one as the Messiah must be ; repentance and remission of sins are proclaimed in His name. This constitutes the fundamental message by the acceptance of which men become disciples—enter the school—of Jesus. There must follow the "teaching them to observe all things whatsoever I have commanded you." By this message the missionaries go into all the world and make disciples— learners, pupils, school-students—of all the nations.

(3) We ought here to sum up certain clear and fundamental implications of this message, which the Scriptures abundantly teach.

(a) The need for the message is universal and absolute because "all have sinned and come short of the glory of God." [1] Only one other truth is so prominently set forth in the Word of God as this ; and it is God's love for these sinners. The sin of Adam and the law of hereditary likeness entailed death upon all men. The first epoch of man's rebellion is sadly summed up in Genesis 6 : 5–6 : " Jehovah saw that the wickedness of man was great in the earth, and that every imagination of the thoughts of his heart was only evil continually. And it repented Jehovah that He had made man

[1] Rom. 3 : 23.

on the earth, and it grieved Him (or He was in grief) at His heart." The outcome of the election of " a peculiar people " is tragically set forth in Isaiah 53, where we see how " All we like sheep have gone astray ; we have turned every one to his own way, and Jehovah hath caused to fall on Him the iniquity of us all."

And the climax of the tragedy of sin is seen in the Christ on the night of Gethsemane. From the upper room of comforting courage He goes to the garden of prayer where all fail Him, even the truest and most trusted followers ; then comes the multitude, piloted by Judas, and we see the Son of Man, betrayed, arrested, deserted and led alone to face condemnation and death, when men " denied the Holy and Righteous One " asking for the freedom of a murderer (taker of life) and killed the Author of life.[1]   Then indeed met the tragedy of sin, the tragedy of ignorance, the tragedy of weakness, all to be overcast with the supreme tragedy of love ; when the lone Christ is led to an accursed cross.

In Romans 1 : 18–3 : 20 the great missionary Apostle demonstrates this universal need for the Gospel " that every mouth may be stopped and all the world may be brought under the judgment of God " that they may be ready for the benediction of " them that hear the joyful sound " of sin's remission.

[1] Acts 3 : 14 f

Jesus' use of the term "*world*" as the antithesis of godliness is a pathetic commentary on sin's wreckage. "He was in the world and the world was made through Him, and the world knew Him not."[1] His world cast Him out as unfit—and still He will not give it up.

(*b*) God has never deserted men, nor any class or race of men; never abrogated His claim, surrendered His control, nor lost His love for them. We must not now take up again the Scripture assertions of this important truth.[2]

(*c*) God's Gospel is designed to be preached in love to all men in all nations. This has been abundantly set forth; but it has never been taken seriously to heart by all God's people. This is the very meaning of the promise and of the gift of the Holy Spirit, whose first work was to make "men from every nation under heaven" hear the glad tidings "every man in his own language."[3] The confusion of the race by sin and pride[4] is to be corrected by the restoration through the Gospel of the Son of God.

2. *The development of the message.*

(1) The clear definite missionary message could not be framed and its proclamation entered upon as the task of believers until the Lord had come and fulfilled all the things written of Him in the divine Scriptures. For the Christ is Himself that

[1] John 1 : 10.
[2] See Chap. II.
[3] Cf. Acts 2 : 1–13.
[4] Cf. Gen. 11 : 1–9.

message.   A Christian propaganda was not possible before the Christ.

Still He found these things written of Himself
when He came, and it was by putting Himself in
relation to these writings that Jesus completed the
message and delivered it to His followers for the
world.   So that in a very real sense God had been
making this message from the beginning of the
race, in His revelation to the race.   A universal obligation could not lie on Israel to evangelize the
world in the Christian sense ; but a right spirit towards all men was needful and obligatory and the
missionary plan must lie, explicit or implicit, in
God's revelation.   Otherwise there were no true
revelation of God's self.   He could not truly reveal Himself to even a few unless that revelation
looked ultimately to all men.   If God would ever
undertake to reach all men that purpose must lie
in, and shape, all His revelations to men.

Further, if when the Messiah comes He is to be
able to justify Himself in His true universal character and work it must be because this idea is
clear in all God's growing word to men.   It was
just this argument that Jesus used, and His Apostles after Him, against the narrow conceptions current in their time.   By this appeal Jesus convinced
the first missionaries, as we have seen.   In the Jerusalem council touching the receiving of heathen
converts [1] Peter, Paul and Barnabas present, as the

[1] Acts 15.

first great argument, that God has clearly done this work and approved it; James then argues from the Old Testament that this is what God has all the time planned to do. So, too, Paul pleads his Gospel universalism on the basis of Old Testament revelation.[1] In making propitiation for the whole world Jesus was in no way overreaching the eternal purpose.

Once more, such an element in revelation is essential to true religion. We have come at length to understand that the elements of a true religion are in their very nature universal and in no way dependent on the accidents of race or place. In teaching men religion God's prophet must reach these spiritual and ethical fundamentals and in so doing proclaim a faith at least potentially comprehending all men. So we find it in the preaching of the prophets of the Old Testament.

And again must we have such true religious teaching and at least some measure of understanding of the teaching to afford a standing place for the inauguration of the Messianic work. An environment and a history make the soil in which shall spring and grow the world-wide movement for redemption. The circle of spiritual believers in the Hope of Israel that we find about the cradle of the Christ are a part of the necessary preparation for an effective cross on Calvary.

[1] See Rom. 15.

Now it will be clear enough that fully to trace the giving and the measure of men's receiving this full revelation of God's love and purpose towards all men would involve examination of the entire Messianic element in the Bible—a subject on which many volumes have been written without exhausting the subject. We must here con tent ourselves with a very summary outline of the facts, seeking to point out what bears most directly on the idea of missions. The universality of God's claim over men and of His redemptive love for men will naturally be written in the Old Testament more largely than is the fact of human agency in making this love known. The latter element finds emphasis in the New Testament.

In comparison with the volume of teaching we find very slight and slow apprehension of the universal claim and love of God to men, and but a meagre measure of sympathy for a gracious purpose towards all.

(2) It will be well to sketch the teaching by historical periods.

(a) Prior to Abraham God deals with the race as a unit. In the meagre Bible record we find little revelation or religion but what there is of both belongs to the race. The first promise of redemption is to "the seed of the woman." [1] When sin has corrupted the whole race a new racial beginning is made in Noah and the cove-

[1] Gen. 3: 15.

nant of God then made embraced all the sons of
Noah "and of these was the whole earth over-
spread." [1]   Thus God's common relation to all
humanity has a history of millenniums as a deep
background for the special dealings beginning
with Abraham.

(b)   From Abraham to Samuel we may designate *the constructive period* of the elect race.   In
the call of Abraham and at each stage of advance
in founding the Hebrew nation several points are
kept clear and distinct :

(i)   Abraham and his seed are to be a channel
of universal blessing.   How this stands out in the
call and covenant of Abraham we have seen.[2]
When Jehovah is about to destroy the cities of the
plain He discloses His purpose to Abraham,
" seeing that Abraham shall surely become a great
and mighty nation and all the nations of the earth
shall be blessed in him.   For I have known him
to the end that he may command his children
and his household after him, that they may keep
the way of Jehovah, to do righteousness and
justice ;   to the end that Jehovah may bring
upon Abraham that which He hath spoken of
him." [3]   When the test of faith came in the offering of Isaac [4] Jehovah renews His covenant and
Abraham becomes " the father of believers " universally ; " in thy seed shall all the nations of the

[1] Cf. Gen. 9 : 1–19.   [2] Chap. II.   Cf. Gen. 12 : 1–4.
[3] Gen. 18 : 18 f.   [4] Gen. 22.   N. B. verse 18.

earth be blessed ; because thou hast obeyed My voice." Abraham's manner of life, his seeming ever to be looking far beyond the mere material possession of Palestine, his intercession for the sinners of Sodom, all indicate that he understood largely the nature of his call. The same end of God's election is set before Isaac : " I will be with thee and bless thee ;   .   .   and in thy seed shall all the nations of the earth be blessed." [1] In the same words is Jacob made to know that the flourishing blessings upon his seed look to the universal good,[2] and Jacob saw the meaning and in prophecy projected the blessing on Judah :

" The sceptre shall not depart from Judah

Nor the ruler's staff from between his feet,

Until Shiloh come (He come whose it is— Syriac)

And unto Him shall the obedience of the peoples be." [3]

(ii) In taking Israel to be His own in a special sense Jehovah is careful to affirm His ownership of all. Israel is His in the midst of other possessions, and His with especial significance for others. This teaching is the first given to the new-born nation at Sinai [4] and is given a new emphasis at the Jordan in Moses' farewell messages.[5] It is easily evident that to Moses was given a large share of the spirit of universalism, and this is the

[1] Gen. 26 : 3 f.   [2] Gen. 28 : 14.   [3] Gen. 49 : 10.
[4] Ex. 19 : 1-5.   [5] Deut. 10 : 12-22.

more remarkable when we recall the many reasons the Israelites had at this time for ungenerous feelings towards other people. Israel is priest among the nations. If she is true to this office all nations will know the glory of Jehovah. If untrue to His religion Jehovah will punish and destroy the nation. Provision is made at every turn for the worship of "the stranger" whom the Hebrew must "love" as Jehovah "loves" him. In the Deuteronomic statements the "stranger" has everywhere "one law" with the "home-born."

If in the times of "the Judges" we find little room to suppose the people had any larger thought of Jehovah than that He might meet their needs we see how sordid was all their conception of religion when "every man did that which was right in his own eyes."

(iii) "All the earth shall be filled with the glory of Jehovah." This is the ground on which Jehovah must punish, even when He forgives, the rebellion of His people.[1]

(c) In *the national period*, from Saul to the Captivity, we pass through the glory and the shame of Israel's national existence and of their religious life. The wide outlook comes into prominence and is grounded upon the principles of spirituality and righteousness which give it a permanent basis. We find abundant teaching of God's universalism in all sorts of relations and all sorts of

[1] Num. 14 : 20 ff.

conditions in the religious exaltation and degradation of "the people of God."

Because of its position in the history and in the
religion of the people, centring as it did in Jerusalem, the passage in Solomon's prayer, dedicating
the first temple to Jehovah, is very remarkable,
wherein he prays : "Moreover concerning the
foreigner, that is not of Thy people Israel, when
he shall come from a far country for Thy great
name's sake, and Thy mighty hand, and Thine
outstretched arm ; when they shall come and pray
towards this house; then hear Thou from heaven,
even from Thy dwelling-place, and do according
to all that the foreigner calleth to Thee for; that
all the peoples of the earth may know Thy name,
and fear Thee, as doth Thy people Israel, and that
they may know that these gates which I have
built are called by Thy name." [1]

In the prophets in this period we find these
teachings :

(i) God's oversight and control of the "nations" and concern for them.   A large section of
Isaiah [2] is devoted to their "burdens"; Amos proclaimed the judgments of Jehovah upon the six
neighbors of Judah and Israel "for three trans-
gressions, yea for four," in exactly the same way
and on the same general principles as upon Judah
and Israel. [3]   And he understands that the children of Israel are as the children of the Ethiopians

[1] 2 Chron. 6 : 32–33.   [2] Isa. 10–30.   [3] Amos 1–2.

unto Jehovah, who brought up Israel out of the
land of Egypt, and the Philistines from Caphtor,
and the Syrians from Kir.[1] Jeremiah understood
his prophetic call to be as " prophet unto the nations " ;[2] and besides frequent recognition of Jehovah's hand upon all peoples,[3] he devotes as
much as one-sixth of all his recorded words[4] to
" The word of Jehovah that came to Jeremiah the
prophet, concerning the nations "[5] in which Je
hovah's relation to these nations is hardly distinguishable from that to Judah. He punishes them
on the same grounds, by the same means and
holds out the same hopes of restoration to some
of them.

These three prophets seem really to understand
God's attitude towards all men in common. Jonah
is destitute of a missionary spirit and the account
of his mission to Nineveh, successfully preaching
repentance to these heathen people, serves not
only to declare Jehovah's attitude of mercy and
concern for all ; but, by contrast with the narrow
spirit rebuked in the preacher, puts especial emphasis on the lesson of love for all.

(ii) There are clear visions of the unlimited
work and universal sway of Jehovah's Servant and
King. Already He is master of the nations and
all must at length own His rule. Even the main
outlines of the course, by which this end will be

---

[1] Amos 9 : 7.   [2] Jer. 1 : 5.   [3] Cf. 18 : 5 ff. ; 25, 27–28, etc.
[4] Jer. 46–51.   [5] Jer. 46 : 1.

realized, are seen already in such passages as
Joel 2 : 28–32 ; Amos 9 : 7–15 ; Micah 4 : 1–5 ;
Zephaniah 3 : 8–10 ; Isaiah 2 : 2–4 ; 19 : 23–25, and
more especially 11 : 1–12 ; 43 : 8–13, and numerous passages in chapters 40–66.[1] That these
peoples from all lands are to come willingly to the
attracting ensign of the Messiah is part of many a
vision of the seers of God.

(iii) The religion of the prophets is of such
quality as makes it independent of nationality or
of election, as the Jews understood election.   In
their religion there is one God supreme over all,
ethical and spiritual in His own character and
in His relations to men, and His demands upon
them ; and He will punish sin, if need be even to
the extent of destroying the chosen people.   Such
a God and such religion are essentially and inevitably universal, and this truth is seen by its
prophets with varying degrees of clearness.

In the Psalms of this period[2] we have also so
much material that we must merely sum up its
main items :

(i) All the ends of the earth and all classes
shall come to the worship of Jehovah, recognizing
His original claim over them.[3]

---

[1] Whether these chapters are to be placed here or during the Captivity, matters nothing for their use in this connection.

[2] Of course one cannot, in many cases, be sure of the date of a
Psalm.

[3] See *e. g.*, **22 : 27 ff.**

(ii) Some set forth the glories of God's universal reign and call for general interest and exertion to bring it to pass.[1]

(iii) Some call the nations to worship Jehovah, predict their coming to His worship; see in the manifestation of Jehovah's glory an impression for good and glory upon all men; and call on Jehovah's servants to make Him known unto all men.[2]

(d) From the Captivity to the Christ is *a period of national subjection*, to characterize it in general terms, during which the experiences and the environment of the Jews led to a modesty of assertion while at the same time they fostered ceremonial and ethnic exclusiveness, and also gave occasion for a more wholesome and exalting influence for religion than Israel had ever exerted before. The expectations developed and cherished in "the Interbiblical Period" do not belong properly to present discussion. From Daniel and from the Temple Prophets, from Ezekiel's vision of the new, restored Jerusalem and the stream of influence flowing from its temple, and from the Psalms of this period we see abundant evidence that Jehovah is keeping before the people still the assurance that His kingdom shall rule over all and that His people shall bless the whole race of men. That the Jews identified God's kingdom with their own dominion is an incidental error very serious

[1] E. g., 72, 47, 65–68, 117.   [2] Study 24, 96, 97, 98, 105.

or them but not affecting the spiritual facts. See Daniel 2 : 36–45 ; 4 : 19–27 ; 7, 12 ; Ezekiel 40–48 ; Haggai 2 : 4–9 ; Zechariah 2 : 3–13 ; 6 : 9–15 ; 8 : 13, 18–23 ; 9 : 9–10 ; 14 : 16–21 ; Psalm 145, especially verses 6, 9–13, 21 ; 148 : 11–13 ; 150 : 6 ; 126 : 2 f.

(*e*) The culmination of instruction in the missionary message came with the ministry of Jesus and of the Holy Spirit, whose function was to recall and enforce the teachings of Jesus and interpret His life, death, and resurrection in their fullest application. The chief office of Jesus during the forty days between His resurrection and His ascension seems to have been to furnish sufficient proofs for witnesses to the reality of His triumph over death and to impress on His witnesses their charge to bear their witness unto all men. Jesus' work was not to spread the Gospel, but to make the Gospel. He indoctrinated the dozen that He might evangelize the millions.

(3) Through all the history of revelation God kept standing proofs that He did not limit Himself to Israel. The head of the elect race found in the Peace-King of Salem one nearer to God than himself and in Abraham all the elect race paid tribute to a man with no ceremonial priesthood but who stood before God as a prophet of peace on earth. Job, of the land of Uz, was God's most trusted servant in all the world in his day. Baalam came from Bozrah with a blessing in his

mouth for Jehovah's people ; Naaman the Syrian
and a heathen widow of Zarephath served Jesus as
examples of God's wider love ; Nineveh stirred
God's pity calling for a preacher of repentance ;
Cyrus and Nebuchadnezzar were moved by God's
hand and did His bidding to chastise and to
cherish His troublesome son, Jacob.   God kept
ever before the eyes of His people the page of His
wider love and the larger meaning of their election.
By word and work He was ever saying :   " The
world is Mine and you are My witnesses to the
world," while to the nations who had dealings with
the chosen people God said :

" Touch not Mine anointed ones
And do My prophets no harm." [1]

We are bound to confess that God's people, for
the most part, miss the meaning of all these high
teachings.   For the bulk of the people and for
most of the time the facts may well be summarized
thus :   An elect race with a glorious Messianic
hope applicable to all the world and entrusted with
a Holy Scripture destined to enlighten all men ;
that race missing the end of its election degrading
its hope until it fails to recognize its Messiah,
hedging about its Scripture till it was accounted a
sin to give it to Gentiles.   Seeking to appropriate
selfishly what was entrusted to them in stewardship Israel lost for an age the power to appreciate
their own heritage.

[1] Ps. 105 : 15.

Against this background of selfishness and in-
tolerance shine brilliant exceptions who, with varying degrees of clearness, fullness, and faithfulness,
comprehend and foster the purpose of God.
These become God's prophets to humanity and so
of the kingdom of heaven.

Under the leading of the Christ Himself, even,
believers are still " foolish and slow of heart to believe all that the prophets have spoken " ; slow to
accept the function of givers rather than getters, of
servants rather than masters, to be in the feast
among men " as one that serveth " rather than sit-
ting in the seats of honor.   Not Israel alone was
slow to see and slower to sympathize with the
divine plan.   Early Christians were slow and
modern Christians slower still and much of the
" Church " since the day of Christ has been un-
faithful to the spirit of Christ.   To win a kingdom
by the quiet way of loving message and the toil-
some way of sacrificial life, while following One
who could exercise omnipotence is not quickly acceptable to men.   Where the Lord would seek
and save, His followers wish to conquer and compel.   On the way to Olivet for the farewell blessing the now commissioned missionaries still wish
to know whether Israel may not now have its
national restoration.[1]   They know by this time
that in the main the kingdom of the Christ is spiritual and so " not of this world " but surely it may

[1] Acts I : 6.

include the restoring " the kingdom to Israel."
They are not ready to make it their whole, sole business to bear witness to Jesus to the ends of the earth.

After Pentecost persecutions must scatter and
evil circumstance compel; visions must lead and
providences prove; and the Holy Spirit must at-
test before Peter and others will see.   Even then
many are convinced without being converted.

It is significant that the first recorded instance
of the arraignment of a member before a church
was Peter for going to Cornelius, and but for his
foresight in providing himself with six good witnesses there is no knowing what the result might
have been.[1]

The lesson was not fully learned even under
Apostolic lead.   A Judaizing, anti-missionary party
arose which was the bane of Paul's life and which
but for that powerful Apostle would have doomed
the new Way to the poor destiny of a Jewish sect.

Late in the century near friends of the Apostle
John suffer exclusion from their church for the
support of missionaries.[2]   Until this day there are
many who for the evangelizing of the world await
the catastrophe of our Lord's return ; many rely
on the movements of God's political providences ;
many are wholly unconcerned.

Through it all some have understood and proclaimed and Christ has triumphed; and will to
the end.

[1] Acts 11 : 1–18.   [2] 3 John 10.

CHAPTER VIII

THE MISSIONARY PLAN

THE essentials of the plan for carrying to the world the Gospel of the Christ we would expect to be given to the witnesses; and we find instructions and guidance at each crucial point. No formal rules are given. That is not the way of the religion of Jesus in anything. His is distinctly not a religion of rules. Against the bondage of the letter He brings the freedom of the Spirit.

Praise God!

1. *The mission fields.*

"The field is the world."[1] "Lift up your eyes, and look on the fields."[2] There is the field within which are the fields. "The whole world lieth in the wicked one"[3] and "the prince of this world hath been judged,"[4] for "To this end was the Son of God manifested, that He might destroy the works of the devil."[5] "This Gospel of the kingdom shall be preached in the whole inhabited earth for a testimony unto all the nations"[6] and of all nations the commission bids us make dis-

[1] Matt. 13 : 38. [2] John 4 : 35. [3] 1 John 5 : 19.
[4] John 16 : 11. [5] 1 John 3 : 8. [6] Matt. 24 : 14.

ciples,[1] and we are to pray for the perfect reign
of God on all the earth.[2] " They that come up
out of the great tribulation and washed their robes,
and made them white in the blood of the Lamb "
are " a great multitude which no man can number, out of every nation and of all tribes and peoples and tongues." [3]

Such is " the imperialism of Christ," the world-
spirit of Christianity wherever it is true to the
leading of the Holy Spirit and in fellowship with
the Lord. In accord with God's claim of all the
earth and His gift of it to His Son, missions bring
" the fullness of the times " when God is entering into His own. But the world is too great a
concept for most minds and presents too great a
task for individual effort or for the instantaneous
undertaking of any organization. For thought
and for effort the field must be divided.

(1) On what principles and lines shall divisions be made?

(a) The primary division is spiritual ; between
that which is " of the world " and that which is
" not of the world." This is the one distinction
drawn by our Lord in His prayer for His work.[4]
Of His missionaries He says, " They are not of
the world, even as I am not of the world," and " As
Thou didst send Me into the world, even so send I
them into the world." So soon as Jesus can say

---

[1] Matt. 28 :18f.

[3] Rev. 7 : 14, 9.

[2] Matt. 6 : 9–10.

[4] John 17 : 14–18.

to one of us " I chose you out of the world,"[1] **He**
has established for that one the deepest of all dis-
tinctions and has laid him under obligation to begin "reconciling the world" unto God.   To begin
with, no other distinction was possible.   All fields
were "foreign" to the life of God.   No distinction
can ever supersede this.   This idea needs constant
emphasis.   No lands are yet " Christian lands "
according to Christ's standards and every servant
of Jesus is in the midst of the first mission field,
" the world."

(b)   "Beginning from Jerusalem," said Jesus,[2]
and Paul's rule was " to the Jew first, but also to
the Greek."[3]   Jesus meant that the Gospel should
be offered first to the Jews, not alone because the
first missionaries were themselves Jews but because
"Salvation is from the Jews" ;[4] because theirs
" is the adoption, and the glory, and the covenants,
and the giving of the law, and the service, and the
promises ; whose are the fathers, and of whom is
the Messiah according to the flesh."[5]   It is not
at all meant that all missionaries in all time shall
first undertake Jewish evangelization ; nor yet, at
the other extreme, that after a brief period of Jewish opportunity they should thereafter be despised
and neglected by the heralds of the Gospel.   If
we may judge from the Apostolic order, we conclude that in every place the Jews are to be

[1] John 15 : 19.   [2] Luke 24 : 47.   [3] Rom. 1 : 16; cf. Acts 13 : 46.
[4] John 4 : 22.   [5] Rom. 9 : 4 f.

offered **their** Messiah, in Jesus, and that the work is quickly to proceed to offering all the Saviour; and that, once He is accepted, there is to be no distinction. When in baptism they have "put on Christ" "there can be neither Jew nor Greek, . . . for ye are all one in Christ Jesus."[1] The distinction is racial but perhaps only superficially so and in reality resting on a deeper principle. The history of the Jew gives God a special claim on him and gives him what should be a special preparation for receiving the Gospel message. These circumstances, however, render him either a quick convert or an obstinate unbeliever and opponent. So when any community of Jews has "thrust the Word of God from them and judged themselves unworthy of eternal life" the missionaries are to turn chief attention to Gentiles.[2] The principle will apply to any class on whom God has bestowed blessings specially preparing them for Gospel preaching.

Peter was Apostle to the Jews but was the first officially to tell the news to Gentiles and his later ministry made no distinction. Paul was the Apostle to the Gentiles but delivered his message first of all in the synagogues and places of prayer of the Jews. Both were led to understand that when men become Christ's, whatever they were before, **they are now "Abraham's seed, and heirs according to** promise."[3] The Jews then must never be neg-

[1] Gal. 3: 27 f.　　　[2] Cf. Acts 13: 46.　　　[3] Gal. 3: 29.

fected nor yet must undue concern for them stay one from spreading the work of Christ where it can win.[1]

(c) A third distinction which is really at the base of the second, and an extension of it, is that between those who have the revelation of God and those who are without it. Who is the Jew and who is the Gentile? What is the deepest difference between them? The contrast which was at first expressed by these terms has for the modern world and modern Christianity its counterpart in the contrast between "Christian" and "heathen" where "Christian" has the most general sense and connotes all who have knowledge of Christ and live in lands nominally Christian. We even carry the term into pagan lands and designate as "Christians" all who have surrendered the pagan worship and who ally themselves with the Christian community even though not personally owning Christ as Redeemer and Lord. In this sense "Christians" know the Christ and approve His teachings, in a general way; "heathen" are "without a Messiah and without hope and without God." If the term "Gentile" be rendered "heathen" it will in almost all cases in the New Testament bring to the modern reader far more nearly the idea intended to be conveyed.[2] We have accordingly so rendered it in our paraphrases

---

[1] Cf. Paul's feeling, Rom. 9 : 1–9, 10 : 1, and his course as a missionary. [2] Cf. *e. g.*, Rom. 15 : 8 ff.

wherever it seemed advisable. One does not of course forget that there **remain** yet many prophecies to be fulfilled regarding the Jews.[1] But the task of our age gets itself better understood if "Christian and heathen" stand for us in place of "Jew and Gentile."

Now there are very many "Christians" who are not yet acquainted with the Christ, or only remotely so as were the Jews at the beginning. To such "Christians" in all communities we must bring the Christ. In Catholic lands and all places where the Christ is hidden under the obscurities of ecclesiasticism, formalism, tradition and priestcraft, there is a people on whom Christ has a claim and to whom He has given a preparation that marks them as the "first" field of missions, corresponding to the Jews at the beginning.

(*d*) Geographical distinction seems to lie at the base of the division in Acts 1 : 8 : "In Jerusalem, and in all Judæa and Samaria, and unto the uttermost part of the earth." Here is not quite our distinction between "home" and "foreign" missions, nor yet that of "city," "territorial" and "general." Not more than one of the Eleven was at home in Jerusalem. Rather are they to begin where they are and gradually to extend their scope until they come to the uttermost parts of the earth. The evangelized territory is not to be abandoned nor left wholly to itself. That is clear enough

[1] Cf. Chap. XI.

But when the cause is established in a centre some are to move on thence to new territory.   Take the case of Antioch, for example,[1] where after Barnabas and Saul have done a large work there and other " prophets and teachers " are at hand, the Holy Spirit takes two of the five—and the great two—for new work while three apparently remain to carry on the work at Antioch.

(2) On what principles shall the missionary select his field, or the mission board ? Remembering always that the whole world is to be reached, that permanent churches must be planted, that the Holy Spirit's guidance is to be had and followed we may learn from Paul three guiding principles, two of which are announced and the third clearly evident :

(a) He will go to people who have not yet heard.   He makes it his ambition to preach Christ so as not to go where He is known already but to fulfill the prophecy that

"They shall see to whom no tidings of Him came,
And they who have not heard shall understand."

This principle hinders the missionary for a long while from going to Rome which he has a great desire to visit but cannot so long as unevangelized territory lies between him and that great city already occupied for Christ.   Even now he can only stop at Rome *en route* to Spain where he can find virgin soil for the Gospel seed.[2]

[1] Acts 13 : 1 ff.   [2] Rom. 15 : 20–24.

It would be a mistake to make this the sole principle in selecting a field. The Moravians may
have erred at this point, seeking not only fields
not occupied but not likely to be occupied. But
one must push on ever towards new territory. The
business of missions is to *extend* the kingdom.

(*b*) Paul made it a point also to labor where
results could be gained. All the early missionaries understood that they were sent to " make
disciples," to get results. They would neither go
nor remain where they found no converts could be
gained. They were to give their witness to Christ
not for the purpose of giving Him a ground to
judge the world for rejecting Him, for He had
said plainly that He came not to judge but to save
the world, nor yet merely to fill up an age of outgathering so that their Lord might return, for they
were sent on a mission of salvation, to turn men
from darkness to light and from the power of Satan
unto God.[1] Luke, as the historian of the first
period of missions, is careful to tell about the results everywhere, a fact that has been extensively
overlooked. No superficial " evangelizing "
could satisfy these missionaries. They must have
power in their witnessing, hence the abiding at
Jerusalem for the promise of the Father. Paul
did not pass on from the Macedonian country until
" from Jerusalem, and round about even unto Illyricum he had fully preached the Gospel." [2]

[1] Acts 26.

[2] Rom. 15 : 19.

(*c*) A third principle was extensively to develop strategic points from which as centres the news might sound forth into all the world. Jerusalem retains the Apostles even when persecution has driven out all others. Antioch holds Barnabas and Saul and engages Silas and others until it becomes a capital city in the kingdom work. Ephesus engages Paul for three years during which " all they that dwelt in Asia heard the word of the Lord, both Jews and Greeks " [1] and the missionary did not stop short of declaring unto them " the whole counsel of God." [2] So of Paul's labors generally, they were in places from which the Gospel would spread. He could thus write a letter to Colossian saints whom he had not seen face to face without violating his principle of intermeddling with no other man's labors. It is easy to find the great centres of influence chosen to erect the lampstands of the world's Light.

2. *The missionary agents.*

We assumed in Chapter IV that the individual Christian believer is the responsible agent in the missionary enterprise and we cited many Scriptures showing how missions appeal to every believer in Jesus. God had one Son. He gave Him as the price of many sons, and each one in his turn the Father dedicates to service in His redemptive work. That this obligatory opportunity lies be-

[1] Acts 19: 10.   [2] Acts 20: 27.

fore the " after-born " as well as the " First-born "
son of God will need no further emphasis.

(1) But in what capacity are believers responsible for the discharge of this mission ? That
some are to be separated from the rest for
special work to which the Holy Spirit has
called them [1] needs no emphasis. But on all
believers rests responsibility directly or indirectly. How does this responsibility come
to the individual ? Four answers are possible,
and each is sometimes assumed.

(a) The General Church—the Spiritual Body
of Christ—may be thought of as conveying the
responsibility to the single believer. There is a
certain mystical truth here but no word of God
locates the responsibility in this Church and for
the reason that in its very nature it cannot be
a source of authority and a centre of responsibility. It has no tangible entity and no organic
life, no material form ; and the mission work
requires definite local habitation and name.
The Church receives and contains all the results
of missions and its glory forms for the believer
a mighty impulse in the work but on him it en-
forces no authority directly.

(b) Shall we find it in the general visible
Church, in a general ecclesiastical organization ?
Where shall we find such an organization,
with central authority ? Theoretically the Roman

[1] Acts 13: 2.

Church claims this but singularly enough has not applied the principle consistently to its mission work. The relation of missions to the Roman Church would prove an engaging topic, but since the New Testament knows no central authority for the churches and the believers we must turn from this.

(c) There are ecclesiastical organizations— churches with administrative functions and some of them exercising legislative functions. In the New Testament these are limited to small areas, usually one city, with autonomous life and independence of action, but without legislative authority. These were extended later to larger territory, then to correspond to the political states with which they were allied. Then came various degrees of separation of Church and State with churches organized with more or less correspondence, geographically, to the political territorial divisions. We may include all these under a single idea—the organized church—whether a local autonomous band or an integrated ecclesiasticism. Is the authority and the responsibility for missions in this body?

One finds no evidence in Scripture of a missionary commission or charge to any church or other organization. The missionary command is found in no epistle to a church.[1] While many

[1] Cf. a full discussion of this in " Three Lectures on Missions " by H. H. Harris, LL. D. ; also, " The Resurrection Gospel," by Robson.

may be ready to question this position on theo-
retical grounds, no church so applies the principle of authority, if we except a few minor
sects. No church can impose upon a member
a specific mission to which he has no conscious
call from God ; while, on the other hand, no
church can relieve an individual from either the
general duty of missionary service or a special
call to specific work. No church would perhaps
now undertake to do either of these things. If
every other member of the church is negligent of
this duty, or opposed to its acceptance, I am still
bound to accept and discharge this duty even
should it result in my excommunication. To this
all will agree.

(*d*) And to agree to this is to say that ultimately the obligation, the responsibility, for missions rests on the individual soul, elect for service
and led to it in regeneration. A redeemed man
is Christ's agent in redemption. So far as the
records teach Philip was the first man to go beyond Judæa carrying the good news of the
Christ. He was in Samaria of his own accord,
under God's leading. At the word of " an angel
of the Lord " he met the eunuch on Gaza road
and " the Spirit of the Lord caught away Philip "
thence and he " was found at Azotus ; and passing
through he brought good tidings to all the cities
till he came to Cæsarea." He was not even
officially a minister and yet was master of his own

missionary movements.[1] True the Apostles **at** Jerusalem sent Peter and John to Samaria to see Philip's converts—the Apostles, mind, and not the church. Apostles have no successors in authority or function. Peter and John felt entirely free, too, without further commission from fellow Apostles to "bring good tidings to many villages of the Samaritans."[2]

When certain men of Cyprus and Cyrene at Antioch brought good tidings to Greeks the Jerusalem Church "did send Barnabas as far as Antioch."[3] What he was to do we are not told. He had no power or authority to silence these free preachers and for more than a year he did not return to Jerusalem, and even then not to make any official report. When he wanted a helper in the great meetings at Antioch he went off, apparently wholly of his own authority, to seek Saul at Tarsus.[4]

It is commonly supposed that it was the church at Antioch that sent out Barnabas and Saul,[5] and yet the church is mentioned only as the location of certain prophets and teachers who had a message from the Holy Spirit as they fasted and prayed, and it was only the Holy Spirit that we can be sure "sent them forth." Nor is there any more evidence of church authority in the report of the missionaries to the church on their return

[1] Acts 8.   [2] Acts 8 : 25.   [3] See Acts 11 : 20 ff.
[4] See Acts 11 : 23–29.   [5] Acts 13 : 1–4.

to Antioch,[1] for the missionaries themselves summoned the assembly and "rehearsed all things that God had done with them" as missionaries do to this day when at home again. They "rehearsed" the same things at a gathering of the church at Jerusalem a little later,[2] and on the way they recounted in "Phœnicia and Samaria the conversion of the Gentiles; and they caused great joy to all the brethren" as always with the story of missionary successes. After a time Paul proposes to Barnabas a visit to "the brethren in every city wherein we proclaimed the word of the Lord." The church was not sending them or asked about it; and when they quarrelled over taking John Mark the question was not referred to the church and each "chose" his own fellow missionary and itinerary.[3] Paul chose his own workers and determined his own movements under the Holy Spirit in all work.

The individual agent directly responsible to his Lord is exactly in accord with the nature of the kingdom of heaven and our relation to it. This accords with the intensely personal and vital method of Jesus in whose religion "each one of us shall give account of himself to God";[4] and with the Lord's teaching that "the good seed" which He sows in the world "are the sons of the kingdom."[5]

[1] Acts 14 : 27. [2] Acts 15 : 4. [3] Acts 15 : 36–41.
[4] Rom. 14 : 12. [5] Matt. 13 : 38.

That "the commission" is to individuals may
well be doubted if we know but one "commission." Paul's commission was clearly personal[1]
and he is careful to maintain this.[2] Peter has
an undeniably personal commission in John
21 : 15–21, where Jesus lays emphasis on individual duty : "Follow *thou* Me." If a corporate
or collective body be supposed at Matthew
16 : 19 ; 28 : 18–20 ; John 20 : 21–23, and Acts 1 : 8,
these will need to be understood in harmony with
the other examples. To conclude the matter
Peter explains the gift of the Spirit on Pentecost
as God fulfilling His promise to give His Spirit
for prophecy to all classes, old and young, sons
and daughters, slaves and maid servants. It is a
common function to prophesy of Jesus.

All Christian duties grow out of the personal
relation to God in Christ ; the duty to be a
witness of the Christ and the duty of membership
in a church which is the working organization of
the kingdom. The individual must not exalt
himself above the church nor segregate himself
from it. All his work should be done as a member of it and with due credit to it. It is the
individual agent who must "hear what the Spirit
says"—but "says to the churches" and even
where a church is wholly lukewarm, and the
Master on the outside, the one member who
hears must open the door and admit the Master

[1] See Acts 22 : 14–21 ; 26 : 15–18.   [2] Gal. 1 : 11–17.

to himself as to one within the church.[1] All honor to the church as the organic working body of servants of Jesus, the Lord.

(2) Let us inquire now what motives impel the missionary agent in his world task. This is answered in Chapters II–VI. All that missions mean in all the relations there discussed becomes the Christian's motives to missionary service. We need not repeat what we studied in those chapters. Christ's motives are the Christian's motives. "The love of Christ constraineth us."[2] Not Christ's love for us, nor our love for Him, primarily, but Christ's love for the world finding its expression in us, is the Apostle's meaning. As Christ was ever drawn forward by a sense of the Father's having sent Him to do this work and by a great yearning for the lost in the world, by zeal for the Father who was dishonored in the world and by compassion for men who knew not God; so we in Christ's place "knowing the fear of the Lord (our fear under Him) persuade men "[3] and "we cannot but speak the things which we saw and heard"[4] whatever may be the "reasons" for or against it.

The command of Christ should be enough, but the impulse of divine life in us by the Holy Spirit is the impelling force. The sense of obligation

[1] Rev. 3 : 14–22.
[2] 2 Cor. 5 : 14. Cf. the entire passage here 5 : 9–6 : 3.
[3] 2 Cor. 5 : 11.   [4] Acts 4 : 20.

lies not so much in objective command as in the spiritual impulse.   We go not in formal obedience to Jesus Christ nor in imitation of Him but in unity of spirit and purpose with Him.

3.   *The missionary methods.*

(1)   " And I, if I be lifted up will draw all men unto Myself." [1]   " This is life eternal, that they should know Thee, the only true God, and Him whom Thou didst send, Jesus Christ." [2]   " Ye shall know the truth and the truth shall make you free." [3] *By what means* shall the Son of Man, once for all lifted up upon the cross, now be lifted up before all men that they may see and " believe that Jesus is the Christ, the Son of God ; and that believing they may have life in His name " ? [4]   Jesus Himself indicated three means by which this result will be accomplished.

(a)   *Attraction.*   He said to the first body of disciples who came into His kingdom :   " Ye are the light of the world.   A city set on a hill cannot be hid.   Neither do *men* light a lamp and put it under the bushel, but on the stand ; and it shineth unto all that are in the house.   Even so let your light shine before men that they may see your good works and glorify your Father who is in heaven." [5]   Christians " are seen as lights in the world, holding forth the word of life." [6]

This means of influence was naturally of primary

[1] John 12: 32.   [2] John 17 : 3.   [3] John 8: 32.
[4] John 20 : 31.   [5] Matt. 5 : 14–16.   [6] Phil. 2 : 15 f.

importance before the coming of Christ. It is
recognized in many Old Testament passages,
and is urged upon God's people as a reason for
faithfulness. The Psalmist sings:[1]

" Jehovah hath made known His salvation :

His righteousness hath He openly showed in
the sight of the nations.

*   *   *   *   *   *

All the ends of the earth have seen the salvation of our God.

Make a joyful noise unto Jehovah, all the
earth."

And the Evangelical Prophet declares: " For
Zion's sake will I not hold my peace, and for
Jerusalem's sake will I not rest, until her righteousness go forth as brightness, and her salvation as a
lamp that burneth. And the nations shall see thy
righteousness, and all kings thy glory."[2] And
again, " Jehovah will arise upon thee, and His
glory shall be seen upon thee. And nations shall
come to thy light, and kings to the brightness of
thy rising."[3]

The same influence is potent for Christianity.
Missions are erecting lighthouses in the world's
darkness. Jesus, His Apostles and the heathen
appear as recognizing this means of extending the
work in the Apostolic period. In modern missions this is becoming a great force, for the lights

[1] Ps. 98 : 2-4.   [2] Isa. 62 : 1 f.; cf. 1 Kings 10 : 1-10.
[3] Isa. 60 : 2 f.

are growing large enough to shine upon "all that are in the house." We have seen how Jesus relies on the union of His disciples in love to make the world know Him.[1] Peter sees that God's "elect race" are designed to "show forth the excellencies of Him that called you out of darkness into His marvellous light," among the heathen, "that, wherein they speak against you as evil doers, they may by your good works, which they behold, glorify God in the day of visitation."[2]

(*b*) *Permeation* is a second means on which Jesus relies for the perpetuity of His work. He taught it by the parables of the leaven,[3] of the seed growing by itself,[4] of the mustard seed,[5] etc. This is the method of life and Christianity is peculiarly the religion of life. It is reproductive, communicative, permeating, vitalizing. Christian history abundantly illustrates this.

(*c*) The *chief means* of the kingdom is *conquest*. Attraction and permeation are inherent in the very nature of Christianity, and not wholly dependent upon voluntary effort, though made more effective by conscious application. But the followers of Jesus are not to sit still and shine, nor to abide in Him and grow; they are missionaries —sent ones—ἀπόστολοι.

The Church must not only shine, but "Arise and

---

[1] John 17 : 20, 23.
[2] 1 Peter 2 : 9, 12; cf. 1 Peter 3 : 1; Phil. 4 : 5; Eph. 5 : 8–11, etc.
[3] Matt. 13 : 33.   [4] Mark 4 : 26–29.   [5] Mark 4 : 30–32.

shine," not only grow but sow as well. Not alone those who see the light and come, or who touch the life and live, but those beyond the radius of the light and beyond the reach of the life power in the saints are to be gained. We must make conquest in the name of our Christ. This is the method of all the statements of the commission and of the aggressive spirit of our Faith. Jesus and His Church are imperialistic. This is the method demanded by the condition of the world. "The righteousness which is of faith" indeed declares that no man need be waiting for some one to go up into heaven or down into the abyss to bring him the Christ; but to every one declares "the word is nigh thee, in thy mouth and in thy heart, that is, the word of faith, which we preach." "For the same Lord is Lord of all, and is rich unto all that call upon Him." But men will not call upon Him till He is preached to them by one sent with the Gospel and proclaiming it with the demonstration of the Spirit and with power. In actual practice "belief cometh by hearing and hearing by the word of Christ,"[1] who has commanded that all shall hear.

Such was the method of the early disciples under the lead of the Holy Spirit. They moved to the task without any plan, on their part, up to the end of Acts 12, though a plan of the Holy Spirit is clear enough. At Acts 13 the Holy

[1] Cf. Rom. 10 : 6–17.

Spirit begins to show His plan to the workers and they follow a more definite order from that time. But with or without a comprehensive plan, wherever they went, or for whatever cause, they went about bringing the good tidings.[1]

And the form of the commission in Matthew is made applicable to all the followers of the Lord, whether technically missionaries or not. There is no formal command to "go." The command is to "make disciples." The "go" appears as a participle. Literally we shall read "Going (as ye go) therefore disciple all the nations (heathen)."

The gifts of the ascended Lord to men through His Church contemplate conquest.[2] Having "led captive a band of captives," whom He had gotten in His ministry, He distributed them as gifts to men. He sends them in four classes (verse 11) all designed to perfect the saints (the whole body of believers) for the work of ministering. These classes of ministers are adapted to the divisions of the world field contemplated for the work:

First we find Apostles. The primary meaning of this (Greek) word is the same as (the Latin) missionaries, and the Roman Catholics have done well in retaining this term for designating their foreign missionaries. We may distinguish in the New Testament two uses of the term if we use "*Apostles*" to render the word wherever the Twelve and Paul are designated in their function

---

[1] Acts 8 : 4; 11 : 19.   [2] Eph. 4 : 8–12.

of *authoritative* founders of the Faith, *e. g.*, Acts
15 : 2, 4, 7 ; and elsewhere, whether applied to
the Twelve and Paul or to others, use the word
"*missionaries*." In this latter sense we find it
in Acts 15 : 8–14, for Barnabas is not an Apostle
and Saul is here submitting his work, not as an
Apostle, but as a missionary, to the judgment
of the Apostles and elders at Jerusalem. So
in 1 Corinthians 4 : 9 Paul thinks that "God hath
set forth us (Himself, Apollos and others, some
of whom are not Apostles[1]) the missionaries last
(lowest) of all, as men doomed to death : for we
are made a spectacle unto the world : both to
angels and men." Whether technically Apostles
or missionaries the word designates founders of
the Faith in new territory—in modern phrase
"foreign missionaries." The foreign missionaries
were usually, if not always, chosen after experience
in home work—established churches, as we see
in the cases of Paul, Barnabas, Silas, Timothy,
Titus ; and in one case, at least, the very ablest,
Barnabas and Saul, were chosen for the new work.[2]

Next come "*prophets*" who speak for God by
special inspiration. They are usually ministers
in the native church, specially endowed for building up the new churches, founded by the missionaries. They held the gift of the Spirit most important for the Lord's work in the new church.[3]

[1] Cf. verse 6.   [2] Acts 13 : 1–3.
[3] Cf. 1 Cor. 14 : 1 ; Eph. 2 : 20, etc.

Evangelists were men who from the strategic centre, where the missionaries have founded a church, evangelize the neighboring districts and extend the work in the province or country where it is already planted. We call them to-day "home missionaries." So Philip in Palestine.[1] Such was the work of Barnabas and Saul in Antioch.[2] Timothy in territory where Paul had already fully preached the Gospel was to "do the work of an evangelist."[3]

Last of all are ministers with the twofold function of *pastors and teachers*, permanent officers for the development and direction of the church in life and service, now that it has become an organ for conserving and developing the kingdom of heaven. In it all we are to bear in mind that all the saints are to be perfected for ministry and that main reliance must be on personal proclamation of the Gospel by the saved upon all opportunities.[4]

(2) We inquire next of the *instrumental agencies* employed in the prosecution of the work.

(a) First reliance was ever placed on the spoken word, the living voice witnessing to the living Christ out of a glowing experience that could not be still, and with a yearning love that could not leave a fellow man alone in sin. So John the Baptist had been a voice crying in

[1] Acts 8, 21 : 8.   [2] Acts 11 : 22–26.   [3] 2 Tim. 4 : 5.
[4] Cf. Acts 2 : 46 f.; Mark 5 : 19 f.; Acts 18 : 26, etc.

the wilderness, and Jesus talked, and spoke, and wept with men, writing no word, but speaking and living the word that shall be written in all tongues and times.

This is the means which Jesus enjoined on His followers and on which He mostly relies;[1] the method which His followers constantly betray the consciousness of having received from their Master.[2] This is the means that lies within the power of every believer and makes it possible to employ in the service of the kingdom the whole body of the redeemed. There is no requirement for formal sermons, nor skilled discourse; no requirement for literary training nor the culture of the schools, nor any lack of fullest scope for the use of these; no need for episcopal ordination or ecclesiastical warrant. This is business for the " unschooled and lay "[3] men as well as for the learned and official. The essential qualification is to have seen and heard and experienced. " I believed, therefore have I spoken " is the Christian's impulse and warrant for his witness to his Redeemer.[4] Such witnesses are vocal and also " living epistles, known and read of all men."[5]

[1] Cf. John 15 : 27 ; Luke 24 : 48 ; Acts 1 : 8 ; Matt. 24 : 14 ; 28 : 19 ; Acts 26 : 16.

[2] Cf. Acts 1 : 21–26 ; 2 : 32 ; 3 : 15 ; 4 : 18–20. 23 ff., 33 ; and see " Apostolic and Modern Missions," Martin.

[3] The real meaning of the words in Acts 4 : 13.

[4] 2 Cor. 4 : 13.

[5] Cf. 2 Cor. 3 : 2 f.

(b)   Miracles were also an agency employed from the beginning to give proof of the nature and character of Jesus and of the relation of His missionaries to Himself.   They constitute one element in the credentials of an Apostle and a mark of divine sanction upon the missionary.   We must not fail to grasp the relation of the miracle to the end of the witnessing—to gain converts to the Christ.   This relation is sometimes overlooked and so needs emphasis.   Miracles were to win converts and Luke is careful to record their success.   The story of the healing of the lame man at the Beautiful Gate of the Temple has its explanation in Acts 4 : 4, where we learn that many that heard the explanation believed and the male believers came now to be about five thousand. The miraculous retribution upon Ananias and Sapphira caused great fear upon all who knew of it ; this was followed by " many signs and wonders wrought among the people " and " multitudes both of men and women," " believing on the Lord, were the more added to them." [1]   The outcome of the healing of Æneas at Lydda was that " all that dwelt in Lydda and Sharon saw him, and they turned to the Lord." [2]   The raising of Dorcas " became known throughout all Joppa ; and many believed on the Lord." [3]   How miracles led to the preaching to Cornelius and his friends and by proving the presence of the Holy Spirit gained their

[1] Acts 5 : 12–14.   [2] Acts 9 : 35.   [3] Acts 9 : 42.

admission to baptism is well known.[1]   Similarly
when some were bold enough to preach to Greeks
at Antioch "the hand of the Lord was with them;
and a great number that believed turned unto the
Lord."[2]   It was the miracle that forced the conviction on Sergius Paulus[3] and on the jailor of
Philippi,[4] and that aided to "make many disciples"
in all the work.   "The signs and wonders," too,
served to guarantee to the Jerusalem council that
God approved the reception of heathen converts
on the missionaries' terms.[5]

The story of the winning of converts in the
Apostles' day is that of "speaking boldly in the
Lord, who bare witness unto the word of His
grace, granting signs and wonders to be done by
their hands."[6]

(c) Apostles and other missionaries made use
of visitation for confirming and extending work
already begun in various places.   Examples of
this appear first in the commission of Peter and
John by the Apostles to visit Samaria where a remarkable work had been wrought through Philip,[7]
and of Barnabas to go to Antioch and see the
work of certain men of Cyprus and Cyrene by
whose word heathen converts had been won.[8]
Again we find Paul proposing to Barnabas : " Let
us return now and visit the brethren in every city

---

[1] Cf. Acts 10–11 : 18.   [2] Acts 11 : 21.   [3] Acts 13 : 14.
[4] Acts 16 : 34.   [5] Acts 15 : 12.   [6] Acts 14 : 3.
[7] Acts 8 : 14 ff.   [8] Acts 11 : 22–26.

wherein we proclaimed the word of the Lord, *and see* how they fare." [1]   "So the churches were strengthened in faith and increased in number daily." [2]   In such work when he could not go himself Paul made extensive use of helpers on various errands as the need might be. [3]

(*d*)   The pen was early and extensively employed in most blessed ways for extending the work.   Some ends could better be served by letters than by personal visits [4] and letters could often go when the missionary was restrained from going. [5]

So we find letters to all the saints in general, to groups of churches, to single churches and to individuals, every one called forth by the opportunities or the exigencies of the missionary work.

In meeting enemies and hinderers, in encouraging and rebuking halting and hesitant believers, in commending the faith to many who would read and ponder, apologetic writings were found useful by the Apostolic missionaries, [6] as in all ages since.

The Synoptic Gospels set down for permanent possession "the matters which had been fully established among the followers of Jesus, even as they were reported by those who from the beginning were eye-witnesses and ministers of the

---

[1] Acts 15 : 36.   [2] Acts 16 : 5.   [3] Cf. Eph. 6 : 21 f., etc.
[4] Cf. 2 Cor. 1 : 15–2 : 4 ; 7 : 8–12.
[5] So Romans, Ephesians, Colossians, Philippians, etc.
[6] So the Gospel and First Epistle of John, Hebrews, 2 Peter.

Word." [1]   So the Gospel facts were preserved for
the saints, furnished to the oncoming missionaries,
and provided a firm historic basis for the missionary religion.   Had these facts been designed
for a restricted or purely national religion they
might have been long entrusted to oral tradition ;
but since they are to be made the possession of
all men they must early be put to record so as to
be introduced as history where they can have no
traditional place. [2]   They constitute a missionary
propaganda as the Acts is the historical exposition of the inauguration of Christian missions.
Translations of the Apostolic writings begin very
early as the natural extension of this means of
propaganda.

There are also writings to encourage and sustain the converts under peculiar trial and temptation and persecution. [3]

(e) The training of missionary workers was
also seen from the first to be essential to the work.
John the Baptist undertook the beginnings of such
training and "the training of the Twelve" [4] was
with Jesus His greatest work. [5]   Paul selected fit
men from all sections where his successes were
achieved and surrounded himself with faithful
men to whom he might commit his message and

---

[1] Cf. Luke 1 : 1 f.   [2] Cf. 2 Tim. 2 : 2 and the entire epistle.
[3] So 1 Peter, Revelation.
[4] See A. B. Bruce's great work with this title.
[5] Cf. John 17 : 8 ff.

who in their turn should be able to teach others also.[1] The training included instruction in doctrine plan and method ; experience in faith, surrender, and self-denial ; practical training in actual participation in the work. For a long while Jesus kept His Twelve under personal supervision and direction ; then came a time when He sent them in pairs to try themselves in work apart from Him, and how eagerly He and they sought opportunity for their report.[2] From that time Jesus devoted Himself increasingly to instructing these men until finally He committed His cause to their hands. Paul pursued the same method and so foreshadowed the missionary training-school which became an institution of missionary Christianity from the second century.

(f) Martyrdom was also a means of missionary extension, taking the term in all its meaning from simple witnessing without hindrance, through all the stages of opposition and persecution to the death of the witnesses for their testimony. Jesus faithfully taught His disciples to expect persecution and death because in the world they should have tribulation and men would even think themselves serving God in killing the witnesses of Jesus. They are warned beforehand so as not to be disconcerted by such experiences.[3] They must

---

[1] 2 Tim. 2 : 2.

[2] Cf. Mark 6: 7–13, 30 ff. and parallel passages in other Gospels.

[3] See John 15 : 27–16 : 4 ; 16 : 33 ; 15 : 20. See also 12 : 23–26.

remember always that the servant is not greater than his master—they must expect treatment similar to that of their Lord. They shall be persecuted in synagogues and prisons, before kings and governors, by parents and friends, Jesus tells them, "for My name's sake." But this will only increase their opportunity for useful service; "It shall turn out unto you for a testimony." They are never to seek primarily personal deliverance but to use the occasion for witnessing: "Settle it therefore in your hearts not to meditate beforehand how to answer; for I will give you a mouth and wisdom, which all your adversaries shall not be able to withstand or to gainsay." By faithful endurance they will gain the end of life.[1] And they rejoiced to suffer for the Lord and with Him for His Gospel's sake [2] from the first imprisonment of Peter and John [3] to the day when in old age John, as "partaker   .   .   .   in the tribulation and kingdom and patience which are in Jesus, was in the isle that is called Patmos, for the word of God and the testimony of Jesus." [4] Paul's catalogues of his afflictions in 2 Corinthians 6 : 4–10, 11 : 23–33, were the common lot of the missionaries so that Paul thought God had set them apart for a sort of universal spectacle.[5] But the

---

[1] Luke 21 : 12–19.

[2] Acts 4 : 23 ff. ; 5 : 41 f. ; 7 : 54–60 ; 8 : 1–3 ; 12 : 1 ff., etc., etc. Cf. also Col. 1 : 24 ; 2 Tim. 2 : 10 ; 1 Cor. 4 : 9.

[3] Acts 4 : 3.   [4] Rev. 1 : 9.   [5] 1 Cor. 4 : 9.

outcome of it was that Christ was proclaimed and in that fact they rejoiced and could not be suppressed in their joy.[1]

(*g*)   Prayer as a means in missionary labor will best be presented in the next chapter.

(3)   Now, how was all this work supported? Whence came the financial backing for the enterprise? This subject, which stands so prominently to the fore in our time, is of so minor importance as to receive scant and only indirect mention in the New Testament. Perhaps, however, this treatment of the subject does not signify so little importance as might at first appear. Money is best gotten indirectly. Indeed, except in such as make it an end in itself, money is used only for gaining that which is the chief matter in one's efforts. Given souls in sympathy with Christ, separated from the world, conscious of responsibility to God and to the world for reconciling the one to the other and what these souls control of material goods in this world will be freely dedicated to the promotion of that kingdom which our Lord calls on us to make the primary object of our endeavor. The Bible prepares the soil of stewardship out of which generous giving for missions will flourish. This is the lesson which missionary leaders are more and more learning. " Seek ye first the kingdom of God and His righteousness and all these things shall be added

[1] Cf. Phil. 1 : 18.

unto you " is the law of kingdom extension for boards and secretaries as well as for missionaries who go to proclaim the message.

There are some important considerations that explain in large measure the slight mention, in the New Testament, of the finances of missions. There were no " home churches " and no " Christian countries " to constitute bases of supply. There were no bodies of strong men, experienced in affairs and in faith to constitute boards and serve as general agents. Jewish Christians, who were the earliest, were as a rule poor and the heathen converts who speedily came to outnumber them were relatively wealthy. The only really large financial undertaking recorded in the New Testament is the collection for the poor saints at Jerusalem,[1] unless we include the semi-communal administration in Jerusalem for the first few years after Pentecost,[2] and this is essentially the same.

As for schools, hospitals, printing plants, houses for worship and other material institutions, about which objection is sometimes urged, it may be said that there is no evidence that the early Christians had any institutions that were not carried into the mission work. In all respects material provisions were largely under the influence of time, place and general conditions which differed largely from those of our day.

[1] 1 Cor. 16 : 1–13 ; 2 Cor. 8–9.
[2] Acts 4 : 32–5 : 11 ; cf. also 6 : 1–6.

We must examine some Scriptural indications as to finances.

In large measure Paul supported himself and those who attended him in work ;[1] but was glad to be free from this necessity. He had a manly independence but he had more time to devote to his mission work when supported. At Corinth he at first worked at tent-making, preaching on the Sabbaths, but so soon as Silas and Timothy arrived from Macedonia he was able to give his full time to the Word.[2] The explanation of this is found in the Epistle to the Philippians where we learn that when Paul departed from Macedonia this church had partnership with him in the matter of giving and receiving and that even in Thessalonica they sent once and again for his need.[3] And we learn further that this was a regular habit of this church, for the Apostle rejoices that from their first day up to the time he wrote them, some ten years later, they had had partnership with him in the extension, defense and confirmation of the Gospel, both while he was in prison and when free.[4] Paul was careful to accept this only as a gift to the cause, not to himself, and to point out that its chief value was to the giving church. He fully recognizes that by the gift the givers entered into participation with his

[1] Acts 20 : 34 ; 2 Cor. 11 : 7 ff., etc.
[2] Act 18 : 1–5 ; cf. 2 Cor. 11 : 9.   [3] Phil. 4 : 15 f.
[4] Such is the clear meaning of Phil. 1 : 3–7.

grace of being a missionary and that the results of
the enlargement of his work on account of their
gifts was fruit that increased to their account.[1]
Thus he encouraged large giving, which was "an
odor of a sweet smell, a sacrifice acceptable, well-
pleasing to God." [2]

Paul took no money from a church or community where he was just now working, founding
a church. In this rule he differed from the other
missionaries and seems to fear that he had made
a mistake in it. The circumstances were peculiar
in his case. He drew so largely on the gifts of
others while at Corinth as to speak of himself as
"robbing" these other churches.[3] Yet he maintains the right of all missionaries to food and
drink for themselves and wives and implies that
this was provided in the case of all but himself
and Barnabas.[4]

While it is contemplated that the body receiving the ministrations of the missionary shall be the
giver it would seem that no effort was made to
maintain any careful distinction. Self-support is
in every way encouraged and fostered, but support beyond self is abundantly evident, and is to
be aimed at.

There are several examples of arranging for
churches to provide for expenses of journeys

[1] Phil. 1 : 7 ; 4 : 17.　　　　　　　　　　　[2] Phil. 4 : 18.
[3] Cf. Acts 20 : 34 ; 2 Cor. 11 : 7–12 ; 12 : 14–18.
[4] 1 Cor. 9 : 3–16.

incident to the mission work. Paul hopes to "make a sojourn with the Corinthian church or even to winter and that they would then set him forward on his journey, wherever he might be going."[1] Meantime Timothy comes to them on an errand and they must see that he is without embarrassment while there and must then set him forward on his journey in peace.[2] By such delicate suggestions he also requests the saints at Rome to provide for his journey into Spain.[3] The Antioch delegation to the Jerusalem Council were "brought on their way by the Church."[4]

The large company going up to Jerusalem with Paul on his last visit had along from Cæsarea "one Mnason, of Cyprus, an early disciple, with whom they should lodge."[5]

Another case of individual support of missionaries is commended especially by John, who takes occasion to point out that we ought to welcome such missionaries who have gone out for the sake of the Name, getting no support from the heathen, since thereby we may become fellow-workers with the truth. He says therefore that one does well to set them forward on their journeys "worthily of God."[6] Thus we come upon the New Testament standard for the financial support of missions—"worthily of God." In manner and measure worthy of God's interest in missions, investment in the

[1] 1 Cor. 16 : 6.   [2] Verses 10–11.   [5] Rom. 15 : 24.
[4] Acts 15 : 3.   [3] Acts 21 : 16.   [6] 3 John 5-8.

cause, blessing on the work, outcome staked on
them ; worthily of God's gift for us and blessings
upon us, and opportunity presented to us, "Worthily of God" is the Christian motto for mission
giving.

The principles of giving to all the interests of
the kingdom are the same and are set forth in
such passages as Acts 4 : 32 ; Philippians 4 : 10–20 ;
2 Corinthians 8–9. "Not one said that aught of
the things in his possession was his own." All
material things are held in stewardship and the
abundance in the hands of Christians in any one
place must supply need at another place. "We
know the grace of our Lord Jesus Christ." God's
gift to Him was "that though He was rich yet for
your sakes He became poor, that ye through His
(material) poverty might become (spiritually) rich."
The Apostle accounts it also a great grace—gift
from God—that by making ourselves poor (materially) we may make many rich (spiritually).
Such giving not only fills up the measure of the
wants of those whom it supports but by being the
occasion of a volume of thanksgiving from very
many it abounds even unto God Himself.[1] No
wonder Paul, in contemplating such an outcome
of Christian giving, exclaims : "Thanks be to
God for His unspeakable gift." [2]

We conclude, then, that as far as possible mission churches were self-supporting ; missionaries

[1] 2 Cor. 9 : 12.   [2] 2 Cor. 9 : 15.

expected support from such as were able to give it; if systematic, sufficient support was lacking the missionaries went on without it, working, suffering, enduring, saving men by means of the Gospel.   Fixed compensation does not appear for any service.   There is abundant evidence in general for the support of missionaries, whether this was true or not of settled pastors.

These days of beginnings leave methods in finances undeveloped; but set forth clearly the principles that call for the consecration of all wealth, intellect, heart, life to the business of witnessing to Jesus in all the world.

IX

THE MISSIONARY POWER

ONE hopes that the student will have felt surprise and disappointment that Chapter III was not followed by a presentation of *the meaning of missions to the Holy Spirit.* Why was it not so? For several reasons a different treatment was decided upon. For one thing, the personal desires and interests of the Holy Spirit are not clearly stated in the Bible. There is very abundant evidence of His personality but few passages give any hint of His personal prerogative, if indeed any do. This is remarkable on first thought, but is quite what is to be expected when we recall His office. Jesus said " He shall not speak from Himself; but what things soever He shall hear shall He speak: . . He shall glorify Me; for He shall take of Mine and shall make declaration to you." [1] True to this function the personal Spirit ever keeps His own personality in the shadow, while making the Christ real to men. It may be questioned whether in Biblical revelation or in believing experience any one has ever been conscious of the Holy Spirit's person. He is like the wind,

[1] John 16: 13 f.

known only by His manifestations and these are most abundant and blessed. When He does His mightiest works we come to know Jesus and Jesus is glorified. We understand Jesus better and know the Father. The Spirit eludes us. To missions the Holy Spirit means everything. And from that standpoint we are to study His work in missions[1] in outline. Following the characteristic of the Spirit stressed by the Lord Jesus we treat of His work as the Missionary Power.

1. The Agent of Power; the Holy Spirit upon and in redeemed men.

"Apart from Me ye can do nothing," is a negative law of the kingdom that the Lord has written before every life of service.[2] "You now understand the Messiah, all His work is committed to you, you must witness for Him unto all the nations; for this you shall have the promise of My Father: but ——" so Jesus calls His disciples up sharply to take heed. "But tarry ye in the city, until ye be clothed with power from on high."[3] No matter how great nor how urgent the work—aye, because the work is so great and so urgent we must lay no hand to it until the Power comes.

(1) If the work is to succeed it must be by

[1] The reader is referred to Dr. Gordon's "The Holy Spirit in Missions."

[2] John 15: 5.   [3] Luke 24 : 49.

the divine power expressing itself through men.
For this, unity of God and man is absolutely required;[1] and this unity is mediated and effected
by the Holy Spirit, and by Him alone. Such is
the command and the promise of Jesus. "Being
assembled together with them, He charged them
not to depart from Jerusalem, but to wait for
the promise of the Father, which, *said He*, ye
heard from Me; for John indeed baptized with
water; but ye shall be baptized in the Holy
Spirit not many days hence." "Ye shall receive
power, when the Holy Spirit is come upon you;
and ye shall be My witnesses."[2] They had heard
from Jesus the promise of the Father in the
upper room and on the journey to Gethsemane.[3]
We have the record in John 14 : 12–29; 15 : 26–
16 : 16 to designate specifically, though in truth
the promise of the Presence runs through all
the speech of that night. We can only sum
up the content and import of this promise. For
the great work entrusted to them the followers
must be able to draw indefinitely on God in
Christ's name;[4] if they are doing this work
Christ will secure that the Comforter shall come
to abide forever with them;[5] He must come upon
working, loving believers for they alone can receive Him;[6] He will bring the abiding, loving

---

[1] John 15 : 1–21; 17 : 20–26.
[2] Acts 1 : 4 f., 8.
[3] Then most fully, not then alone.
[4] John 14 : 12–14.
[5] John 14 : 15–16.
[6] John 14 : 17–19.

presence of the Father and Son to the man who loves Jesus and keeps His word; [1] the full meaning of this cannot be known until the Comforter has come when He will teach all things, recall all Christ's teaching, and bestow the peace of Jesus; [2] the glory and purpose of the Father are to be fulfilled in the perfect, joyous, fruitful service of Jesus' followers in oneness with Him; [3] the real, dominating, determinant purpose of the Spirit is to bear witness to Jesus, and believers are witnesses along with Him; [4] the witness of believers is to be in an unfriendly, opposing, persecuting world, a world dead to be awakened; rebellious to be subdued; selfish to be surrendered; and for this the presence of the Spirit is more serviceable than the bodily presence of Christ, for by His presence each one on whom He comes becomes a divine agent in convicting the world in respect of righteousness, sin, and judgment; [5] much remains to be taught the men who are to do Jesus' work and the time and conditions prevent teaching it, but the Spirit of Truth will guide into all the truth, taking Christ's things and showing them to His servants. [6]

It is of the utmost importance that we remember that the Holy Spirit does all this by coming "upon you," the loving believers who have accepted the work of the Christ: not upon the

---

[1] John 14 : 20–24. [2] John 14 : 25–29. [3] John 15 : 1–25.
[4] John 15 : 26 f. [5] John 16 : 1–11. [6] John 16: 12–16.

world, which cannot receive Him, nor in the world as an unrecognized and so impersonal force; but upon you. This is the word of Jesus. This is not meant to deny the extensive, indirect work of the Spirit; but to emphasize that His direct work for the kingdom is in and through believing, surrendered men. "Apart from Me ye can do nothing" is the negative warning of which the counterpart is spoken first : " He that abideth in Me and I in him, the same beareth much fruit," for "If ye abide in Me and My words (message) abide in you, ask whatsoever ye will and it shall be done for you." [1]

When witnessing under most difficult circumstances, not the human witnesses but the Holy Spirit will be the speaker, speaking in us.[2]

(2) This is the Power by which Jesus Himself accomplished His work.

Even His generation is attributed to the Spirit. Matthew tells us that Mary "was found with child of the Holy Spirit," [3] and Luke [4] reports the angel as saying to Mary : "The Holy Spirit shall come upon thee, and the power [5] of the Most High shall overshadow thee ; wherefore also the holy

---

[1] John 15 : 5, 7.　　　　　　[2] Mark 13 : 11.
[3] Matt. 1: 18.　　　　　　　[4] Luke 1 : 35.
[5] Should we not read Power ? Whether it is a name or a description, the use of the term is significant. In the Hebrew parallelism here it really seems better to take it as a synonymous name and read " even the Power of the Highest " and the absence of article in the Greek tends to the same conclusion.

thing which is begotten shall be called the Son of God."

At His baptism the Holy Spirit comes upon Him to abide,[1] convincing John the Baptist, in accordance with a revelation from God, that this is the Messiah.[2] Into the crucial, initial conflict with Satan Jesus, full of the Holy Spirit, is led by the Spirit[3] and from the temptation He returns "in the power of the Spirit into Galilee."[4]

When Jesus came to preach in Nazareth we find Him claiming in Himself the fulfillment of the prophecy beginning, "The Spirit of the Lord is upon Me."[5] From the study of Isaiah, as well as in His own experience, Jesus could not but be deeply impressed with the Spirit's relation to the Messiah.

Isaiah had foreseen that the Shoot out of the stock of Jesse, the fruitful Branch, should have the Spirit of Jehovah resting upon Him, for wisdom, understanding, counsel, might, knowledge, and reverence for Jehovah, making Him remarkable for His intuition[6] of God, faithfulness, righteousness and authoritative judgment. Thus shall the Root of Jesse be made an ensign unto the nations which shall seek unto Him, and His resting place (the end of His work) shall be glorious.[7]

Jehovah points Him out: "Behold My servant whom I uphold; My chosen in whom My soul

---

[1] Matt. 3: 16 f.; Luke 3: 21 f.   [2] John 1: 32–34.
[3] Luke 4: 1.   [4] Luke 4: 14.   [5] Isa. 61: 1.
[6] Hebrew "scent."   [7] Isa. 11: 1–10.

delighteth ; I will put My Spirit upon Him ; and
He will bring forth justice to the nations ; " [1] and
the Servant Himself, declaring His eternal work,
announces that " now the Lord Jehovah hath sent
Me, and His Spirit." [2]   Matthew [3] shows how
Jesus was fulfilling Isaiah 42 : 1 ff., and how when
Jesus was charged with being in league with
Beelzebul He claimed to cast out demons " in the
Spirit of God." [4]   Jesus then went on to discuss
the sin of speaking against the Holy Spirit which
shall not be forgiven in this age nor that which is
to come, for this is " an eternal sin." [5]   Mark says
that this teaching was " because they said He hath
an unclean spirit." [6]   Peter declares that it was
part of the current teaching about Jesus, " pub-
lished throughout all Judæa," that God anointed
Him with the Holy Spirit and with power : who
went about doing good and healing .   .   .   for
God was with Him." [7]   " The Spirit of Holiness" by which Paul says Jesus was " declared to
be the Son of God in power, by the resurrection
from the dead " [8] was none other than the Holy
Spirit through whom Luke again tells us Jesus
gave to His Apostles whom He had chosen the
commandments touching His kingdom and their
service in it.[9]

---

[1] Isa. 42 : 1, a most striking parallel to the occurrence at the baptism of Jesus.

[2] Isa. 48 : 16.   [3] Matt. 12 : 15.   [4] Matt. 12 : 28.

[5] Matt. 12 : 31 and Mark 3 : 29.   [6] Mark 3 : 30.

[7] Acts 10 : 36-38.   [8] Rom. 1 : 4.   [9] Acts 1 : 2.

John 3 : 34 has a word, most probably from
Jesus Himself, which we are accustomed to
apply, after an interpretation in the King James
version, to Jesus alone, but which is true of the
whole work of the Lord : " He whom God hath
sent speaketh the words of God ; for He giveth
not the Spirit by measure." The application of
this measureless gift is indicated in Isaiah 59.
Here Jehovah explains that the deplorable condition of Israel is due to sin (verses 1–15) ; and,
seeing in grief that there is no justice among men
and no intercessor, He determines by His own
hand to bring salvation and make universal the
fear of His name (verses 16–19) ; then "a Redeemer shall come to Zion " (verse 20) and under
Him this covenant shall be made : " My Spirit
that is upon thee, and My words which I have
put in thy mouth, shall not depart out of thy
mouth, nor out of the mouth of thy seed, nor
out of the mouth of thy seed's seed, saith Jehovah,
from henceforth and forever" (verse 21).[1] This
is one expression of the promise of His Father
which Jesus sends upon His servants.

(3) The conscious fellowship with the Holy
Spirit and dependence upon Him in their witnessing is everywhere evident on the part of the New
Testament missionaries. The priority and pri-
macy of the Spirit in this work Jesus pointed out[2]
and His followers understood. It was He who

[1] Cf. 44 : 3 ; 32 : 15.   [2] John 15 : 26 f.

gave demonstration and power to their preaching,[1] and whose working in us in power guaran-
tees all our success;[2] who distributes in sover-
eign wisdom the " gifts " that make for effective
growth.[3]

Dr. Pierson has called the Book of Acts " The
Acts of the Holy Spirit," and the name has
eminent appropriateness. It may equally be
called " The Gospel of the Holy Spirit." Those
who have received the good news of Jesus and
His salvation to proclaim to the world found it
good news for their mission when the promised
Spirit's presence could be announced, and it is
a gospel which many of us need to hear and
accept that we may be workmen with no cause
for shame. Yes, Acts tells us of what Jesus, who
had " begun to do " so much in His own person,
continued in the person of the Holy Spirit through
the missionaries. The feature of the Divine Presence is never lost sight of in the entire story. He
made Pentecost[4] with all it contained, and inaugurated the Gospel age; filled them all again that
they might speak the word with boldness when
they met persecution;[5] was lied to by Ananias
and Sapphira;[6] stirred Stephen to service and
emboldened him;[7] wrought new work in Philip;[8]
came upon Saul at the hand of Ananias;[9] led

---

[1] 1 Cor. 2 : 4 f.   [2] Col. 1 : 29; cf. 1 Cor. 3 : 5 ff. ; 4 : 20.
[3] Rom. 12 : 3–8; 1 Cor. 12 : 4–11.   [4] Acts 2.   [5] Acts 4 : 31.
[6] Acts 5 : 1–11.   [7] Acts 6–7.   [8] Acts 8.   [9] Acts 9.

Peter and Cornelius in the opening of the door of faith to the heathen and set His seal upon it when open that it might no more be shut;[1] raised up prophets for the work;[2] opened, through an angel, the prison door for Peter;[3] inaugurated a new and general era of mission work;[4] and attended the missionaries in their work;[5] settled a serious question affecting the growth of the kingdom;[6] restrained, guided, blessed Paul and his associates in work;[7] when Paul found certain disciples at Ephesus not yet acquainted with the Holy Spirit and baptized them in the name of the Lord Jesus the Spirit approved with signs;[8] He led Paul at every stage of his career.[9] Not one chapter in this Book is lacking in record of the Spirit's work of guidance, strengthening, making the witness effectual in conversion, planning and directing the movements of the missionaries. Truly His was the power " energizing mightily " in them that bore the good tidings to men.

2. *Prayer is the means by which the Power of the Spirit is brought* upon the witnesses of Jesus.

The relation of prayer to every work of the kingdom is essential and insistent. We must

---

[1] Acts 10–11.   [2] Acts 11 : 27 ff., etc.   [3] Acts 12.
[4] Acts 13 : 1 ff.   [5] Acts 13 : 4–14 : 27.   [6] Acts 15 : 28.
[7] Acts 16 : 6–10, 14 ; 17 : 34 ; 18 : 9 f.   [8] Acts 19 : 1–7.
[9] Remaining chapters of Acts show this.

pray for the Power, pray in the Spirit, pray at every phase and every turn of our witnessing. Our prayer must be the submission of ourselves to the Spirit and the bringing ourselves into sympathy with the mind of the Spirit who is the Witness over and within the witnesses.

(1) It was a good day in the history of the training of His disciples when "it came to pass as Jesus was praying in a certain place, that when He had ceased, one of His disciples said unto Him, Lord teach us to pray." [1]   It indicated that *the connection between prayer and power in the life of our Lord* was impressing itself on their minds.   And the memory of that disciple went back and placed a new significance on an earlier experience, as he added, "as John also taught his disciples."   The addition shows that the Forerunner who was "filled with the Holy Spirit from his mother's womb" laid stress on prayer in his preaching of the kingdom.

We shall do well to make diligent study of *the prayer life of our Lord.*   It is significant that the incidents of His birth and first years move in an atmosphere of devout communication with God. His first recorded word is "Did you not know that I must be in My Father's house?" [2] and He de-

[1] Luke 11 : 1.

[2] Luke 2 : 49.   The substantive is not in the Greek, but the context shows that only this word can be the first meaning, though a larger meaning is doubtless to be understood also.

clares later that He regards His Father's house as
" a house of prayer." [1]

It was while Jesus, after His baptism, was praying that the heaven was opened and the Holy
Spirit descended upon Him and a voice came out
of heaven saying, Thou art My beloved Son ; in
Thee I am well pleased.[2] We recall in this connection that the three occasions when the Father
spoke audibly His approval of His Son in His
earthly ministry were all while He was in prayer.
When He went into the mountain where He was
transfigured before the three the only recorded
purpose for that ascent is that " He went up into
the mountain to pray." And Luke's record follows : "And as He was praying the fashion of
His countenance was altered . . . and there
talked with Him two men, who were Moses and
Elijah. . . . And a voice came out of the
cloud, saying, This is My Son, My chosen ; hear
ye Him." [3]   Again in the last days of His ministry
Jesus, standing at the point where His Gospel
can no longer be confined to Jews but must become universal and so realizing that He must
now " be lifted up " prays, " Father glorify Thy
name. There came therefore (N. B.) a voice out
of heaven : I have both glorified it and will
glorify it again." [4]

When His work was growing so great in

[1] Luke 19 : 46.   [2] Luke 3 : 21 f.
[3] Luke 9 : 28–36.   [4] John 12 : 28.

Galilee "it came to pass in these days, that He went out into the mountain to pray; and He continued all night in prayer to God. And when it was day, He called His disciples; and He chose from them twelve, whom He also named Apostles."[1] No more important act belongs to all the plan and work of the Lord's mission and He comes to this selection only after a whole night of prayer. A while later, when His compassion is greatly stirred for the shepherdless multitudes, Jesus calls these prayer-appointed men and says, "The harvest indeed is plenteous, but the laborers are few. Pray ye therefore the Lord of the harvest, that He send forth laborers into His harvest": then after this call to prayer He gives instructions to the twelve and sends them out to meet in their measure the needs of the multitudes.[2]

When His days were crowded with throngs eager for His healing Jesus would arise a great while before day and seek a quiet place for prayer;[3] when a sordid, selfish multitude would "take Him by force to make Him king," "He departed into the mountain to pray" and joined His disciples rowing in the midst of a raging sea "about the fourth watch of the night";[4] facing death and distress in His friends with bitter, running hate in His enemies, at the tomb of

[1] Luke 6: 12 f.
[3] Mark 1: 35.
[2] Matt. 9: 36–10: 5.
[4] John 6: 15; Mark 6: 46–48.

Lazarus, He lifted up His voice to thank the
Father that He had heard Him [1]—heard Him no
doubt when several days ago across the Jordan
came the word of Lazarus' illness.   Then, showing the fact and faith of His prayer habit, He
adds, "And I knew that Thou hearest Me always ;
but because of the multitude that standeth around
I said it, that they may believe that Thou didst
send Me." [2]   Then it was a petition for power
over death, now a prayer of thanksgiving to inspire faith, always it is the prayer of trust.

When Satan asked for the Twelve that he might
sift them it was important to allow him to do his
worst, but Jesus tells Simon "I made supplication
for thee that thy faith fail not." [3]   When the
climax of His life came and He was meeting the
cross our Lord forever sanctified a place and an
experience when He "poured out His soul unto
death" in the prayer of Gethsemane and was
"heard for His godly fear." [4]   So He came to His
cross in prayer, and continued to utter prayer [5]
until He gave His spirit into the Father's care. [6]

And what lessons in prayer He taught His followers in word, as well as in His own praying.
As soon as they understand their function in the
kingdom they must make their chief prayer for
the kingdom ; [7] and it will be His own request

[1] John 11 : 41.   [2] Verse 42.   [3] Luke 22 : 31.
[4] Heb. 5 : 7.   [5] Luke 23 : 34 , Mark 15 : 34.
[6] Luke 23 : 46.   [7] Matt. 6 : 9 ff.

that the Father send the Other Presence to abide with them.[1]

Well may the witnesses learn that men " ought always to pray and not to faint," [2] and come with the request of the early disciples, " Lord teach us to pray." Then let us go and learn the full meaning of the limitless prayer promises to them that undertake the Lord's " greater works." [3]

In our work of binding and loosing on earth for heaven Jesus has a final message : " Again I say unto you, that if two of you shall agree on earth as touching anything that they shall ask it shall come to pass for them from My Father who is in heaven. For where two or three are gathered together in My name, there am I in the midst of them." [4]

" All things whatsoever ye pray and ask for, believe that ye received (at the time of asking) and ye shall have them." [5]

(2) The history of the power of the witnesses, in Acts, shows that the Power in the witnesses came in connection with prayer.

The great initial and permanent advent of the Spirit on Pentecost followed ten days after the Ascension. How these days were spent we may read in Acts 1 : 12–14 : " Then returned they unto Jerusalem from . . . Olivet. . . . And when they were come in, they went up into

[1] John 14 : 16.   [2] Luke 18 : 1.   [3] John 14 : 12ff.
[4] Matt. 16 : 19f.   [5] Mark 11 : 24

the upper chamber where they were abiding.
. . . These all with one accord were applying
their strength to prayer." While they were still
thus together in one place came the powerful
manifestation "and they were all filled with the
Holy Spirit."

After the first experience of persecution the disciples all came together in prayer for courage and
power. "And when they had prayed, the place
was shaken where they were gathered together;
and they were all filled with the Holy Spirit, and
they spake the word of God with boldness." [1]
When Peter and John came down to Samaria
and saw the converts Philip had gained "they
prayed for them that they might receive the Holy
Spirit. . . . Then they laid their hands on
them and they received the Holy Spirit." [2]   Cornelius and Peter was each at prayer when there
came to them the remarkable revelations that by
bringing them together opened the door of faith
to the heathen. [3]   "Behold he prayeth" was the
ground on which Ananias is sent to Saul of Tarsus
in Damascus that he might receive his sight and
be filled with the Holy Spirit. [4]   When the angel
had delivered Peter from prison and he came to the
house of Mary he found many gathered together
praying; prayer had opened the way for power. [5]
It was while the "prophets and teachers" at Anti-

[1] Acts 4 : 31.   [2] Acts 8 : 15 ff.   [3] Acts 10 : 2 f., 9.
[4] Acts 9 : 11, 17.   [5] Acts 12 : 12.

och "ministered to the Lord and fasted" that "the Holy Spirit said, Separate Me Barnabas and Saul for the work whereunto I have called them." [1] It was at "a place of prayer" that Paul and his fellows made their first converts in Europe,[2] and on their way to "the place of prayer" that they cast out the demon from the demoniac girl [3] and while Paul and Silas "were praying and singing hymns unto God" that the earthquake loosed the bands of the prisoners and led to freeing the souls of many.[4] Philippi was acquainted with the Gospel through prayer and in power. But enough illustrations have been given to show how in practice the power came with prayer.

(3) To complete the presentation, glance at the stress the great missionary Apostle puts upon intercessory prayer as a force in his work. We need not now attend to the numerous exhortations to prayer running through his epistles, except so far as they relate to the progress of kingdom extension. We have seen already the earnest and comprehensive nature of his prayers for the fullness of God to be realized in the Church.[5]

Already in 1 Thessalonians he asks the brethren to pray for him and his associates [6] while in 2 Thessalonians he amplifies the request:[7] "Brethren, pray for us, that the word of the Lord

---

[1] Acts 13 : 2.   [2] Acts 16 : 13 f.   [3] Acts 16 : 16.
[4] Acts 16 : 25–34.
                                              [5] Eph. 1 : 15 ff.; 3 : 14 ff.
[6] 1 Thess. 5 : 25.
                                              [7] 2 Thess. 3 : 1 f.

may run and be glorified, even as also with you; and that we may be delivered from unreasonable and evil men."

To the Corinthians he tells how he has been delivered from death by God "on whom," says he, "we have set our hope that He will also still deliver us: ye also helping together on our behalf by your supplication; that for the gift bestowed upon us by means of many, thanks may be given of many persons on our behalf." [1] They were to help God deliver Paul by praying to that end and so the gift would come upon him by means of many and God would be glorified in the gratitude of many. To the Romans his plea is most urgent and solemn: [2] "I call you on, brethren, through our Lord Jesus Christ and through the love of the Spirit to strive together with me in your prayers in my behalf unto our God, in order that I may be delivered from the disobedient in Judæa, and that my ministration which is for Jerusalem may be acceptable to the saints; that I may come unto you in joy, through the will of God, and with you find rest." This request follows immediately upon his outline of his missionary principles and plans.

In each of the four letters from Rome, where he was in prison, he expresses his desire for, and reliance on, the prayers of his brethren.

[1] 2 Cor. 1: 10f.   [2] Rom. 15: 30 ff.

He hopes to be allowed to come to Philemon "through your prayers.' [1] He knows that the opposition and trouble he is encountering shall turn out for the accomplishment of the purposes of his ministry through the petitions of the Philippian saints for him and " by the supply of the Spirit of Jesus Christ " [2]—a highly suggestive combination, intercessory prayer for the missionary and the supply of the Spirit of Jesus Christ.

All the many addressed in the Ephesian letter are urged to make supplication " on my behalf, that utterance may be given unto me in opening my mouth to make known with boldness the secret of the good news, for which I am an ambassador in a chain, that I may be emboldened as I must speak." [3]

He exhorts the Colossians to lay themselves out in prayer with watchfulness and thanksgiving, "praying at the same time, also, concerning us, in order that our God may open to us a door for the word, to talk the secret of the Messiah, for which indeed I am in bonds, in order that I may make it manifest as I ought to speak." [4] He tells them, moreover (verse 12), how their pastor, Epaphras, is ever " striving for you in his prayers, that ye may stand perfect and fully assured in all the will of God."

[1] Verse 22.
[2] Phil. 1 : 19.
[3] Eph. 6 : 19 f.
[4] Col. 4 : 2 ff.

Thus the Apostle commits to intercessory prayer every interest of the missionary cause.

The divine order in this work is: hear the call to witness; surrender for this service; learn that the power is all of Christ; believe in the Lord and in this work; pray always for the power of the Spirit; labor incessantly in His strength.

"Ye shall receive power after the Holy Spirit is come upon you." [1] "If ye then, being evil, know how to give good gifts unto your children, how much more shall the Father who is of heaven give the Holy Spirit to them that ask Him?" [2]

[1] Acts 1 : 8.   [2] Luke 11 : 13.

X

THE MISSIONARY WORK

THE work of missions as presented in the Bible belongs to two periods, one before and one after Christ.

1. *In the period of preparation.* During this period there were few who understood the spirit and end of the kingdom and their whole efforts were needed to hold Israel's head above the deluging waters of heathenism and against the current of awful depravity of sin. And the world message was not yet framed, nor could be until it could be written in the Redeemer's blood and read in the glory of His resurrection. Kingdom growth could not now be by conquest, except by little here and there; and what was gained by attraction and done by permeation it would be difficult to trace with any show of accuracy. It is better to treat the entire period and its work in its truest aspect, as preparatory to the Messiah and His missions.

It will be needful, too, to rely on the implications of Scripture, which might be confirmed and expanded from general history, rather than on explicit citation for much that belongs to the preparation for a new age of God's plan—the age of grace and truth. The numerous expressions of the constant claim of the Bible to God's control of the forces and peoples of history and direction of all to the ends of His kingdom justify and require that we study the missionary preparation outside, as well as in, the chosen race. That "ethnic movements are missionary" has been well set forth by Dr. Barnes,[1] among others; and the Scriptures could not be otherwise interpreted. It will illustrate this use of all nations if we examine it in the two Gentile nations in which the preparatory work culminated and then point out the more specific missionary work by and through Israel. Prophets of such a preparation—prophets of Jehovah God—are the men who bring their fellow men to truer conceptions of God; of human sin and spiritual need; of individual worth; of ethical values, and of religious motives and destiny. Such prophets arose in various lands and times, Persians, Hindus, Romans, Greeks.[2]

(1) *Material preparation* is illustrated in the Romans, though they also aided in other ways. We may outline their value to missions thus:

(a) The Roman Empire greatly aided in the practical conception of racial unity. "The world" came to be a synonym for the Roman Empire, and the term is so used repeatedly in

---

[1] "Two Thousand Years of Missions Before Carey."

[2] Cf. Wenley, "Preparation for Christianity in the Ancient World"; Hyde, "From Epicurus to Christ," etc.

the New Testament.[1] A universal kingdom was the right time and place for *the universal religion* to be inaugurated and to send out the missionaries of its universal kingdom. One law for all mankind and one Lord of lords and King of kings was an easy conception when missions began.

(*b*) The Roman power provided religious toleration while the coming together of all sorts of men from all parts of the world empire in its capital gave opportunity for a sort of study of comparative religions, all of which conduced to the sense of need and opportunity for appeal for the best, and ultimately for the final, religion.

(*c*) The Roman Empire was also used to cast up an highway for our God through all its wide borders. The maintenance of peace in all the provinces and the wise accounting of every province an integral part of the empire and not a mere dependency gave a solidarity to the whole people, a community of interest and a cosmopolitan publicity of affairs that made it possible for the Christian missionary to appeal to common knowledge of the Christian facts, for they were not done in a corner.[2] The facilities for travel, for intercourse and commerce of ideas, the security and encouragement for all who had occasion to go where they might wish, were never equalled in the world before this time, and after the fourth century never again until in the past century.

[1] *E. g.* Luke 2 : 1.

[2] Acts 26 : 26.

(*d*) It was under Rome's prosperity, too, that man's incapacity for making himself a sufficient religion became manifest, as did also the vain effort by sinful luxury and licentious abandon to dismiss the concerns of the soul. In Rome all the cults of the age, the mysteries, the sorceries, the necromancies, the polytheisms, hero-worship and apotheosis of imperial masters, all had their opportunity and their judgment.

(*e*) A language for the good tidings in all western Europe was added to the facilities for the heralding of the good tidings.

(*f*) The material contributions of Rome were positive and indispensable. The spiritual preparations we have mentioned were negative. One other positive value came also in the fact that it was Roman law and jurisprudence that provided the thought forms for the Christian doctrine of righteousness. These had to be modified and a new significance put upon them for the new divine facts involved, but the forms of thought are those made familiar by Rome's methods of judicial procedure.

(2) The Greeks were the intellectual missionaries of the age just preceding the coming of the Christ and illustrate for us God's use of such means in advancing His kingdom, both before and after the hegemony of Greek thought.

It is a commonplace that when Rome made material conquest of Greece she in turn became subject to Greek intellectual control. In each case God was taking away from each the vineyard and delivering it to another bringing forth the fruits thereof.[1] So He has used the nations all through history.[2]

(*a*) Greece was the world's teacher of the place and value of humanity in this world. The Sophists first of all took man for the centre of study and the standpoint for knowing things; Socrates showed that the moral nature is the real thing in man, with conscience as the voice of Divinity; the ethical dramatists taught men to look for moral judgments with awards and penalties on the basis of a moral order dominant in the universe; and Plato saw that the religious element in man is the supreme fact and longed for the coming of some Divine Man who could teach the way to harmony with God. The Hebrew prophets proclaimed all these truths, or assumed them, but it was from Greece that their sound went out among men.

(*b*) The Greeks taught men to think, to think deeply and accurately. When they were made the world's intellectual teachers they were distributed throughout the world that they might fulfill their mission. Christianity is not a system of thought but it uses thought and appeals to thinking men and offers problems for the best and highest thinking. The influence it gained with

[1] Matt. 21 : 41.   [2] Cf. Isa. 20 ; Dan. 7, especially verses 14, 26 f.

Greek thinkers and the early influence of Greeks in Christian education fit exactly into this view.

(c) Greek thought produced Greek skepticism which undermined the religion of Greece with its mythology and superstition and discounted the heathen gods. It could not proclaim the true God for to it He was the Unknown God, but the needful God. Without Him there were not gods enough in Athens, even when it was easier there to find a god than a man.

(d) Greeks provided missions a universal language, highly perfected, and, because of the thought history of the people, with a vocabulary wonderfully fitted for religious universalism, idealism, and ethical values. At the same time this language was largely emptied of religious content by virtue of Greek skepticism and the words were perfected vessels ready to be filled and sanctified with religious meaning. Much of the preaching and nearly all the writing of Apostolic missions employed this tongue.

Remember now that we have spoken of these two nations as illustrative of a sort of indirect, but not non-essential, work for kingdom extension in which the people have served the God of heaven who in the days of these kings is setting up His kingdom which shall never be destroyed.[1]

(3) Our main concern is with the religious preparation which made use mainly of the Hebrew

[1] Dan. 2 : 44.

people. We must outline the mission work accomplished through them.

(*a*) What was done was in the main indirect and undesigned on the part of Israel. In spite of their deplorable apostasies, their low ideas and corruption in religion and life, their rebellion against Jehovah and unfaithfulness to the ideals He gave them, it must still be remembered that relatively Israel's moral and spiritual influence was usually for the bettering of the nations. Their racial integrity was based on a religious principle and supported by a religious history which was a never-failing source of appeal for reforming king and prophet of righteousness. When the people had sunk so low that they were not better than their neighbors, when the cup of their iniquity was full and they must pay the penalty of national captivity and ruin, the prophets of Jehovah were sent to make it clear not only to Israel, but to all the nations as well, that this calamity was not due to the impotence of Israel's God but to the holiness of His nature which made it morally impossible for Him to perpetuate the wicked nation even though it could call Moses and Samuel to stand before Him and plead the covenants and history.[1] So it came about that the loss of national standing by the missionary race was made occasion for emphasizing their religious message to all men. The prophets of the apostasy were at once the

[1] Jer. 15 : 1 and cf. Ezek. 14 : 14, 20.

prophets of the holiness of God and of His message to all men. Such were Isaiah, Amos, Jeremiah, Zechariah and Daniel in peculiar degree. So long as the racial integrity was preserved Israel was inevitably a teacher of their ideas of God and His goodness; and when that integrity was threatened and falling, then flourished the greatest prophetic period in their history. When other nations fell it was understood to be a failure of their gods but Jehovah took care to make Israel's fall the sign of His power used in the interests of His purity and the lesson of religion had its widest reading under most impressive circumstances.

So it was that Jehovah's presence and power manifest in Israel, and His ethical and spiritual superiority to all heathen conceptions of deity, made constant appeal to men. The value of such an appeal is recognized in many places in Scripture. Take, for example, the exhortation of Psalm 98 : 2 ff. :

"Oh, sing unto Jehovah a new song;

For He hath done marvellous things :

His righteousness hath He openly showed in the sight of the nations.

He hath remembered His loving-kindness and His faithfulness towards the house of Israel :

All the ends of the earth have seen the salvation of our God.

Make a joyful noise unto Jehovah, all the earth;

Break forth and sing for joy, yea sing praises."
Similarly all of Psalm 67, from which this :
" God be merciful unto us and bless us,
And cause His face to shine upon us ;
That Thy way may be known upon earth,
Thy salvation among all nations."

That this was an effective influence we find
examples in the whole course of the history.
Abimelech came with his captain-general to say
to Abraham: "God is with thee in all that thou
doest," and to make a covenant with him for
generations and to seal it by oath of Abraham's
God, both of them.[1] And the same reverent fear
was shown of Isaac because of God's protecting
presence with him.[2] The strategy of the Gib-
eonites by which they gained a place in Israel's
life was not highly moral but speaks of the fame
of Jehovah's name and His works in behalf of His
people.[3]

The influence of David's career and of Solomon's beginning so impressed Hiram King of
Tyre that when Solomon sent him a message
asking help in building the temple and had said,
"And the house which I build is great ; for great
is our God above all gods. But who is able to
build Him a house, seeing heaven and the heaven
of heavens cannot contain Him ? " Hiram feels
no resentment but replies : "Blessed be Jehovah,
the God of Israel, that made heaven and earth,

[1] Gen. 21 : 22 ff.   [2] Gen. 26: 26 ff.   [3] Josh. 9.

who hath given to David a wise son . .
that should build a house for Jehovah, and a
house for His kingdom." [1]   It requires no stretch
of imagination to find here an indication of a very
extensive influence for the religion of Jehovah.
How extensively aliens were attracted to Israel's
territory is intimated by the use made of them in
preparing for the temple building by both David [2]
and Solomon, the latter employing as many as
153,600 of them. [3]   We need not assume devout
piety for all these and their families any more than
for all Israel but they were certainly under the
spell of Jehovah's religion.

It was " when the Queen of Sheba heard of the
fame of Solomon concerning the name of Jehovah"
that "she came to prove him with hard questions."   And this fact informs us that Solomon's
fame was bound up with Jehovah's religion and
we learn that the queen understood that He was
a God of love, justice and righteousness. [4]   The
very wide influence of Israel under the reigns of
David and Solomon gave very exceptional opportunities for educating the world in true ideas
of religion, and we have seen in some of the
Psalms how this opportunity was appreciated.

Even in days of depression and national in-
consequence there were opportunities for influen-
cing the heathen.   Naomi quietly won Ruth to

[1] See 2 Chron. 2.   [2] I Chron. 22 : 2 ff.
[3] 2 Chron. 2 : 17 ff.   [4] I Kings 10 : 1–10.

her God while a refugee in Moab.[1]   Rahab saved
herself and family by her insight and faith.[2]
These two heathen women and a third, wife of an
Hittite, Bathsheba,[3] entered their blood in the
genealogy of Jesus, thus giving the heathen a
natural possession in the Saviour of the world.[4]
The captive maid in Naaman's household did[5]
what many another may have done.   What
may have been the influence of the great body
of Israelites who did not return from Babylon
and other lands in which they were scattered can
only be conjectured.   There are those who think
their influence discernible to this day in preparation for the Gospel in the East.

The restored Jews entered upon a period of
religious influence quite remarkable when we
consider their small number and very subordinate
national position.   They returned with a subdued
spirit, a chastened religion, an intense exclusiveness and a new intensity of future expectancy
that made them notable among nations.   The
literature of this period indicates a large and
growing influence of Jewish religious ideas on
the thought of the world.

(b) Of direct, conscious and purposeful missionary effort we cannot recount very much.
The law provides for the reception and treatment of converts but the records do not show

---

[1] Ruth 1: 16 ff.   [2] Josh. 2: 8 ff.; 6: 22 f.
[3] Matt. 1: 6.   [4] Matt. 1: 5 f.   [5] 2 Kings 5.

efforts to win these nor the accession of any great numbers. A famous instance is that of Moses' successful persuasion of Hobab to accompany the people of Israel from Midian to Canaan.[1] Some of the Psalms, notably such as 65 and 66, are universal in spirit and application and may well have been designed for use by many others than Israel. Such songs in the days of David and Solomon, of Hezekiah and Josiah would be heard and sung by many a "stranger within the gates" and might have larger use still. Ecclesiastes is a very powerful sermon, with the subject "The End of Man," reached in the close where the preacher exclaims: "The end of the matter; all hath been heard: Fear God, and keep His commandments; for this is the whole of man. For God will bring every work into judgment, with every hidden thing, whether it be good or whether it be evil."[2] If Solomon was the author of this masterful work it is likely to have been widely read and its adaptation is unlimited.

Jonah was an unwilling missionary and the spirit of the man is the only real argument against its historical character. But, however unwilling, he was remarkably successful in bringing the great city of Nineveh to repentance and saving it from its doom. Possibly the ungracious spirit of the preacher intensified

---

[1] Num. 10 : 29; cf. Judges 4 : 11.   [2] Eccl. 12 : 13 f.

his severity and heightened the alarming effect of his warning. In any case he presents a remarkably informing incident in Israel's career.[1]

That Isaiah and Amos had messages for others than Israel we have already seen,[2] but we have no record of the results of their messages to the nations.

Jeremiah was called to be a prophet not of his nation merely but "to the nations" and the records tell of his messages to many peoples. In the main, however, he was for these, as for Israel, the prophet of Jehovah's punishments.

After the Captivity the land was filled with a degraded and ignorant mixed multitude sent from various places to occupy the land. When wild beasts distressed them they applied to the King of Assyria who sent them one of the Hebrew priests to "teach them the law of the god of the land." He was a Samaritan and perhaps not very orthodox or godly. At any rate his work was far from thorough. The immediate result is summed up by saying: "So these nations feared Jehovah and served their graven images;" yet they laid the foundation for the Samaritan variation of the religion of Jehovah.[3] The Samaritans came to cherish the Messianic

---

[1] Cf. Matheson, "Representative Men of the Bible."
[2] Chap. VII.   [3] 2 Kings 17: 24–41.

hope and were many of them prepared for the good tidings.[1]

Daniel, in a ministry covering practically the whole period of the Captivity, was called upon to stand before the four great kings in succession. He maintained a true and courageous course through it all and spoke with fearless faithfulness to the kings of Jehovah's moral laws and judgments, of kingly pride and sin, and of the manner in which Jehovah rules above the kings, lifting up and casting down. His ministry was wonderfully successful. Nebuchadnezzar's proclamation "to all the peoples, nations and languages, that dwell in all the earth" recounting his dreams, his experiences and Daniel's wisdom from God, tells how when he was restored to reason, " I blessed the Most High, and I praised and honored Him that liveth forever; for His dominion is an everlasting dominion, and His kingdom from generation to generation. . . . Now I, Nebuchadnezzar, praise and extol and honor the King of heaven ; for all His works are truth, and His ways justice; and those that walk in pride He is able to abase." [2]

To the same effect is the brief decree of Darius "that in all the dominion of my kingdom men tremble and fear before the God of Daniel; for He is the living God, and stedfast forever, and

[1] Cf. John 4 : 4–42 ; Acts 8.   [2] Dan. 4.

His kingdom that which shall not be destroyed;
and His dominion shall be even unto the end."[1]
Cyrus seems to have come under the favorable
influence of Daniel and then to have been especially kind to Ezra.   In the first year he issued a
proclamation allowing all Jehovah's people who
cared to to return to Jerusalem and reëstablish the
worship of Jehovah.   In this decree he recognizes
Jehovah thus: "All the kingdoms of the earth
hath Jehovah, the God of heaven, given me; and
He hath charged me to build Him a house in
Jerusalem, which is in Judah."[2]   The king provided for materials, for the safe conduct of the
pilgrims and for their protection in the land of
Judah.

Artaxerxes[3] in his turn aided and protected the
Jews under both Ezra and Nehemiah as did
Darius[4] in his turn.

We take all these accounts together as indicating the fidelity of many witnesses of Jehovah
during the days of their darkness and of God's
sanction and blessing on them in giving them
favor in the eyes of the mighty.   How many came
to believe in the God of Israel or how intelligently
and consistently they believed it is not possible to
say.   Some large measure of light certainly fell
on the world from Jewish religion in the days of the
Babylonian and Persian empires.   It is likely that

---

[1] Dan. 6 : 25 ff.   [2] Ezra 1 : 2.
[3] See Ezra and Nehemiah *passim.*   [4] Ezra 5–6.

the " wise men from the East " who sought the King in His cradle were the successors of noble converts of this early day.   And one thinks that the purity of Zoroastrianism must owe much to such men as Daniel who was accounted the wisest man in all the land because "the spirit of the holy gods " was in him. [1]

After the Restoration begins the period of most active efforts by Jews to win converts.   The motives are mixed; partly for removing the burden of reproach by making their position understood; partly pride of their better religion and ethics; partly the stubborn zeal of mere proselyting; partly zeal for the God of Israel; partly the hope of hastening the day when Jerusalem should rule the earth as many believed: of love for men one finds very little.

The persistent struggle for separate existence as a people, located, as they were in Palestine, upon the very highway of the nations made the Jews "a city set upon a hill " whose light could not be hid.   The various kings, and especially Ptolemy Philadelphus, distributed the Jews in companies throughout the whole land and so what light they carried shone into every corner. The very nature of their religious ideas, so radically different from all other religions, made it inevitable that they should attract attention.   Alexandria became the centre of a definite literary

[1] Cf. Dan. 5 : 11.

propaganda. There their Bible was translated into Greek and came to be widely distributed, and when Jesus was born one of the most famous Jewish writers, Philo, was sending out weighty writings seeking to make the Jewish faith appealing to men of Greek learning.

In various ways and by many means it came about that in almost every place bands of devout proselytes were attached to the worship in Jewish synagogues and these were the readiest hearers of the good news brought by the missionaries. We find them at every turn in Acts, in individuals, like Cornelius, and in groups as at Thessalonica, Beræa, etc. They passed readily over from Jewish hope to Christian realization.

2. *In the period of progress* we have only the first century and our New Testament records tell little of the outcome of the work beyond the seventh decade of the century. All our study has had to do with various phases of this progress and it remains here only to study what we find indicating the extent of the work and its results.

(1) The work of Jesus and of John the Baptist was limited in scope to " the lost sheep of the house of Israel." John attracted enormous multitudes and aroused the interest and expectancy of all the Jews in Palestine. Paul's finding at Ephesus [1] certain disciples who had been baptized " upon the baptism of John " indicates that from John went

[1] Acts 19 : 1 ff.

forth some to distant places preaching the coming of the kingdom of God and baptizing those who accepted the message.   But John is soon followed by Jesus after whom John's disciples in part go. Jesus did not take these over bodily nor as a matter of course.   They voluntarily accepted Him as their Messiah or Teacher, and it would seem that by no means all John's converts were ready at once to accept the Messiah.

Jesus never aimed at mere numbers, and from the first could not trust Himself to some who professed to believe in Him.[1]   At times, especially in Galilee, He was all but overwhelmed with the multitudes, more or less interested, and from various motives.   They came even from beyond the borders of Palestine.[2]   But when material and sordid hopes began to realize that they were doomed to disappointment in Jesus, and when His enemies pressed hard upon His disciples as heretics, then came a great thinning of the ranks [3] and towards the end there were not many who felt called on to face the difficulties and dangers of following Him.

After the sifting of motives and the testing of faith, even after the encouragement of the Resurrection, there were only somewhat "above five hundred" to meet the Lord on the appointed mountain in Galilee to see and hear Him.[4]   And

[1] John 2 : 23–25.
[3] John 6, etc.
[2] Matt. 4 : 24.
[4] I Cor. 15 : 6.

of all these we find but "about a hundred and twenty "[1] who accepted the discipleship of service and went to the upper room in Jerusalem to await the promised Power for witnessing. He had laid the foundation, made the atonement, imparted His Spirit to a small number of men. These had His attitude towards the Father and towards men and towards the world order As He stood with them at the parting on Olivet He showed them a world and sent them to feed its hunger and save its life just as He had sat upon the slope of a hill on the eastern side of Galilee's lake and blessed the bread and fish and then, breaking it, had given it to the disciples to set before the hungry thousands. His success consisted in making a few men so understand and share His Spirit that He could live and labor in them. This is ever the measure of success in His work.

(2) After Pentecost for three or four years we have a period of "beginning from Jerusalem," laying the foundations, discovering the power of the Gospel and the spirit and task of its message.[2] Then for six or seven years there is the period " in Judæa and Samaria," within which there is gradual, progressive and undesigned passing through the confines of Judaism and over into the world of humanity, regardless of religious forms and history.[3] After this the Gospel is cut loose from its Jewish base and enters upon its career as

[1] Acts 1 : 15.   [2] Acts 2–7.   [3] Acts 8–12.

a world force, reaching out " unto the uttermost parts of the earth." [1]

When we undertake to measure the labors and results we are powerfully impressed with the meagreness of record and paucity of data. We have no account at all of nine Apostles ; none of Barnabas and Mark after they part with Paul ; most of the years of Peter's ministry are unrecorded, and of thousands of workers we know nothing. Tradition scatters the Apostles and other workers over nearly the whole of Asia and North Africa, while the course of history follows only the wake of the labors of Paul and others in Europe. The names of countries — " every one under heaven "—represented in the Pentecost audiences indicate an almost immediate distribution of men with knowledge of the Gospel over all the limits of the Roman world and bordering lands in the East. Naturally the Twelve would follow the converts into these lands for confirming their faith and extending their labors. Then, too, the fact that so many of the Hebrew race remained in the interior of Asia would draw in that direction men who were to preach to the Jews first the word of life.

The hints in the New Testament are verified in profane history to the effect that by the end of the Apostolic age the Roman Empire was well planted with witnessing stations, churches of Christ, extending south as far as Ethiopia

[1] Acts 13-28.

and east as far as the Hindu Kush and the
Caucasus Mountains. That India and China
were entered in this period is possible but no
extensive planting of the Faith in either is
probable. So much for geographical extent.
The numerical measure cannot be determined.
There are numerous notes in the early chapters
of Acts, but these grow indefinite and we are
soon reading of "multitudes both of men and
women," "a great company of men, and many
even of the priests," "of the devout (proselyte)
Greeks a great multitude, and of the chief
women not a few,"[1] of "many . . . also of
the Greek women of honorable estate, and of
men not a few,"[2] etc., etc.

By A. D. 60, the Roman Government no longer
confused the Christians with the Jews, as a
mere sect, but recognized their separate entity
and found them so numerous that it thought
it advisable to check their growth. Already
they must have numbered from a quarter to a
half million. Tens of thousands died under the
Neronian and Diocletian persecutions. By the
end of the century their numbers are variously
estimated at from two to five millions in the
Roman Empire, with a goodly number, possibly, beyond its limits.

As a social power the Christians became an
early and growing factor in the life of the people.

[1] Acts 17: 4.　　　　　[2] Acts 17: 12.

We are accustomed to think that God's order in converting a people is to begin with the lowest orders of society and work upward. This assumption has not been sufficiently questioned. The truth is rather that there is no specific order in the social scale. Paul could say that in Corinth "not many wise after the flesh, not many mighty, not many noble" were among their number,[1] but he could also write from Rome, "All the saints salute you, especially they that are of Cæsar's household."[2] Luke is careful to tell us that very many of Paul's converts belonged to the leading classes. Professional religionists and men of pride in social position or learning were not won in great numbers, though Paul is himself an exception here, but neither would it be true to imagine that the bulk of early Christians belonged to the class of ignorant, degraded and poor. "The lewd fellows of the baser sort" usually combined with the Jewish elders and Pharisees to withstand the work of the missionaries, and the converts came from that sober, serious middle class who constitute the strength of any community and every movement that wins. The chosen Apostles of the Lord were not technical students nor men of great material possessions, yet Matthew was a man of means, James and John left their father with the hired servants when

[1] 1 Cor. 1 : 26.   [2] Phil. 4 : 22.

they forsook their fishing for discipleship, Peter was able to entertain Jesus in his house at Capernaum, Nathaniel was a distinguished Israelite, and the Zealot had won a name for political activity. The "publicans and sinners" who found in Jesus so good a friend were not all thieves and harlots. The terms only mean that they were without religious standing in the critical orthodoxy of the synagogues of that day and Jesus had as little standing there as had these followers. "The common people" who "heard Him gladly" were just the plain, simple-hearted people with no religious pride to spoil and no religious standing to lose, open to God's message and ready for God's salvation. And as it was in Jewry so it was in all the world. A Nicodemus and a Joseph of Aramathea stood at one limit, a dying robber on the cross and "a woman that was a sinner" at the other limit and from one limit to the other God called in the Gospel of His Son, and all who answered were saved; the great majority were of the middle class who really belong to no class. This fact needs thought.

Out of all proportion to their numbers the Christians are, before the end of the first century, exerting great influence and power for the renovation and elevation of social life. Many, including the authorities, still regard them with suspicion and hatred but they have become in great measure the light of the world and the salt of the earth.

(3) It will be proper very briefly to summarize the reasons for such rapid growth in this period.

(*a*) First of all is that material, intellectual and spiritual preparation of the world for missions which we have set forth so inadequately in this chapter. When God is preparing to send the message He is preparing hearers for the message. This is one of the first lessons of New Testament missions.

(*b*) The enthusiasm of Christians for their new faith helped. They were free from the forms and traditions of religion, unhampered by the dignity of order, the restraint of precedent, or the reserve of propriety. At first their religion was in all respects personally accepted and every element of it was matter of individual experience. Children were not yet "born into the Church" nor did they inherit a faith implicit in many things that might never become explicit in their intelligent belief. Such a faith was vital in every man and strong to project itself through him. As far as possible we must restore and maintain these conditions in each generation if we would have generations of Christians mightily impelled to missions.

(*c*) There was everywhere immediate contact with the world to be evangelized. There was

Very Important

no such distinction as " Christian lands " and
" heathen fields." So far from needing to seek
a field for service no New Testament Christian
was able at all to escape the heathen. They
pressed in upon him at every turn. His work
was ever ready to his hand, and he must teach
the other man or be corrupted by him. The same
condition exists still so soon as we recover the
true idea of witnessing for Jesus. Remembering
that all are born unregenerate and that no land or
district is yet in the full sway of the kingdom, our
work is as near as that of the saints at Antioch
and Philippi.

(*d*) Persecutions kept the churches purified.
There was no worldly gain of any sort to be had
for professing the Name. Only those whom
God's Spirit had touched would have reason
for adding themselves to the bands of Jesus'
witnesses. We live under other conditions and
must strive after that purity of church membership which was largely provided automatically in
the days of the Apostles. And we may remember that even then many who were unworthy did
get in, alas for the weakness of human nature !

(*e*) Missions were then on the heart of every
Christian. To this end were they called. Election was for service and not for selfish congratu-
lation. That is a very significant fact recorded
in Acts 11 : 26 where it came to pass " that the
disciples were called Christians first at Antioch."

"Were called" represents a Greek word [1] quite different from what one would expect. It means "were called after their business" as one names certain men "bakers" or "tailors." They were given the business name of Christians. If that could only be forever a business name all the world would soon at least know that there was "opened a fountain for sin and uncleanness."

No limitations were laid on the layman in proclaiming the Christ. All were witnesses and to the end of this period it was accounted that any man may be essentially a prophet for "the testimony of Jesus is the spirit of prophecy." [2]

[1] χρηματίσαι.   [2] Rev. 19: 10.

XI

THE MISSIONARY CONSUMMATION—PROPHECY OF MISSIONS

IF we raise the whole question of the outcome of missions and the manner and order of events in that outcome we shall set for ourselves a task not merely impracticable but altogether impossible. An entire volume, the size of this, would not be sufficient for stating fully all the schemes of prophecy that have been set out by prophetic students of all degrees of patience and care, as well as of imaginative fancy and constructive genius.

1. *Theories of the progress and outcome of the Gospel age and of the manifestation of the King in His glory.* Here we can do no more than to group, by the principle of general likeness, into four classes the innumerable views on this subject. Truly there are as many schemes as writers, and a great many more, for there are many who give themselves to scheme-making for the kingdom who have not been able or disposed to commit them to print; and no two such students have been found to agree in the details of the " plan of the ages.'

(1) Foremost of all we would place the class who designate the *present age* as the age of the Church, the Ecclesia, or of Outgathering, or of Election. All these terms are regarded as practically synonymous designations of the chief fact of the age. It is also called the Age of Witnessing, but this term cannot properly be appropriated by any class of expositors since witnessing is so clearly the method of missions under whatever theory one may hold as to their outcome. Only when the word is used in a narrow sense can it be so appropriated. Unfortunately it seems so to be employed by some, as if the function of the Gospel were to witness to a few of each nation that God might save them under certain conditions, but in the case of the majority to prepare for using this message as a basis of condemning them. Such an idea is so unworthy of God and so utterly at variance with God's declared desire that all might come to repentance and salvation,[1] and Christ's declaration that He was not come to condemn the world but to save it,[2] that one wonders greatly that good men should ever have thought of witnessing in this light. To represent the Gospel as laying the foundation for condemning the great majority of men mistakes the nature of man, already condemned, and the nature of God, seeking to save.

Returning to the theory in its most general

[1] 1 Tim. 2 : 3–7, etc.   [2] John 12 : 47.

comprehension, it maintains that relatively few are
to be saved in this age.   Then will come the age
of the kingdom, the millennium, with Satan bound
and the universal work of salvation under the
personal reign and direction of the Messiah.
Whether the agents of the Christ in saving the
world are then to be all Christians, the Church ;
or the Jewish nation, redeemed ; or the Jews and
martyred Gentile saints then reigning with their
Lord on earth, there is much difference of opinion.

It is also a question among those of this view
whether the age is to become genuinely Christian
or only nominally so.   Again is there difference
as to whether the Christ will reign in person or by
a Deputy, and whether this age will issue in the
completion of the work of redemption and the
turning over of all to the Father, or will be suc-
ceeded by another age of Messianic reign.

Support for the general character and result of
the present missionary period is found in such
passages as Mark 13 : 26 f. and Acts 15 : 14 ff.
"Then shall they see the Son of Man coming in
clouds with great power and glory.   And then
shall He send forth the angels, and shall gather
together His elect from the four winds, from the
uttermost part of earth to the uttermost part of
heaven."   That these "elect" shall be only a few
from each nation is, however, a hardly legitimate
inference, especially in view of Jesus' own treatment of the question "Are there few that are

saved?"[1]   He declined to discuss that but insisted on the most earnest effort to enter in.

James said before the Jerusalem Council:[2] "Symeon hath rehearsed how first God visited the heathen, to take out of them a people for His name.   And to this agree the words of the prophets ; as it is written,

After these things I will return

And will build again the tabernacle of David, which is fallen ;

And I will build again the ruins thereof,

And I will set it up :

That the residue of men may seek after the Lord,

And all the Gentiles (heathen nations) upon whom My name is called,

Saith the Lord, who maketh these things known from of old."

Two uses are made of this : First : James' expression " visited the Gentiles to take out of them a people for His name " is supposed to convey the idea that God's plan in this age is to visit all the nations and take out of each a few for Himself while for the most part they remain in sin and death ; second : James is supposed to have given an outline, in the quotation from Amos 9 : 11 f., of the successive stages of the scheme of the ages, which involves, (a) "visiting" for election of Gentiles while Jews remain untouched for the

Luke 13 : 22 ff.   [2] Acts 15 : 14–18.

most part ; (b) restoration of the Jews to Jerusalem ; (c) conversion of the Israelites ; (d) the evangelization of the rest of the world ; (e) the consummation of the age. All these items except the first are to be after Christ's return.

It would seem however that James understood His words to mean Jehovah's return, in the Messiah, for a work that was to include Jew and Gentile ; for the purpose of James was the very practical one of justifying the work of Barnabas and Saul and reaching a Christian conclusion as to the proper requirements to be made of converts from heathenism.

One might refer to many authors here but it will be sufficient to mention the very admirable and useful course of lectures on " The Holy Spirit in Missions " by the late Dr. A. J. Gordon.

(2) There are a great many who seem to assume that all the work of missions is to precede the second coming of our Lord and the millennium. There is to be a gradual growth of the kingdom of heaven until that time when the results of the age of witnessing, together with the effects of a cataclysmic demonstration, will be gathered together under the personal reign of the Christ. Something like this seems to be involved in the thinking of the large majority of those who speak upon missions and conduct them. It cannot be said, however, as is true of the first class, that the views are the result of any definite and sustained

effort to determine the exact outcome, or the order of events especially as to the millennium. Indeed it is quite common, though less so than formerly, to hear the advocates of missions say that "We have nothing to do with results," it being our duty to carry the Gospel to all men, leaving the outcome wholly with God.

The general progressive character of the work of mission conquest in this age is sustained, besides several prophecies, by the parables of the leaven, the mustard seed, the seed growing of itself, the tares, etc.

(3) A third view is in harmony with the evolution theories which, in all spheres of learning, dominate the thought of our time. According to this view, by the long processes of evolution the spiritual forces at work in society, ethics and religion will ultimately gain control and dominate the earth and thus will be brought in the "new heaven and the new earth wherein dwelleth righteousness." No effort is made to sustain this view by specific texts of Scripture, though the claim would be made by many that the spirit of the Bible is at least not out of harmony with such a view. It is frankly admitted that this is not consistent with the common Christian belief in the possible imminency of the return of the Lord to the earth, for the second coming is practically eliminated from this theory. For a brief but very clear and frank stating of this position, as well

as for a very admirable discussion of some phases of missionary science the reader is referred to Clarke's " Study of Christian Missions."

(4) One more view, or attitude, towards this question must be taken into account. There are very many who do not feel that it is safe or satisfactory to undertake to work out any detailed schemes for the progress of the ages; they cannot even find that there is any certain teaching as to the relation of the millennial age to the missionary duty and task, nor even as to the nature and duration of the millennium. They yet feel that the work of missions has a very great bearing on all the plans of God with reference to the race; expect great results in the moral and religious reformation of the race through the Gospel, accounting it the power of God unto salvation of Jew and Gentile and on no small scale; and they hope that the climax of the missionary age will be the coming of the Lord the second time, apart from sin, but still, as at the first Advent, unto salvation,[1] while at the same time they do not undertake to say what will be done in this new age for the salvation of men. The parables of the kingdom, the prophecies of the Messianic rule, the commands and promises of Christ seem to this class, so far as our missionary duty and expectation are involved, to have to do with the present Gospel age. They find their horizon

[1] Heb. 9 : 28.

marked out as in Paul's injunction to Timothy:
"I charge in the sight of God and of Christ Jesus,
who shall judge the living and the dead, both by
His appearing and His kingdom; preach the
word, when there is good opportunity and when
there is no opportunity."[1]   Paul places here two
great events, the Advent and the Judgment, between which lies the kingdom, so far as our
preaching introduces it.

2.   Among all these views we come to inquire,
*What can we know from the prophecies as to mis-
sions?*

Certainly we can know something.   To His
friends Jesus has made known all that He heard
from the Father,[2] and Paul reveals to us something of the plan of the ages which God laid down
in Christ Jesus,[3] and Jesus sends the Holy Spirit
to teach His missionaries all things, to remind
them of the teachings of Jesus, to guide into all
truth and to declare things to come.[4]   It is not
clear to what extent the Spirit will announce "the
coming things" *beforehand*.   He will interpret at
the time much, surely, as Jesus did.

When we begin to seek in Revelation for the
answer to our question we find two classes of
Scriptures: plain open teaching which is often
directly related to the missionary task and oppor-

---

[1] 2 Tim. 4: 1 f., an effort to render the exact meaning of the original
[2] John 15: 15.   [3] Eph. 3: 11 and context.
[4] Cf. John 14: 26; 16: 13.

tunity imposed by our Lord ; apocalyptic teaching which leaves room for limitless latitude of interpretation, and the interpreters have exercised great liberty here.   The limits of our chapter warn us not to undertake to invent a new theory, or decide among schemes which can be wrought out from apocalyptic utterances only by means of cryptographic keys which vary with all the interpreters and where each key opens up a different scheme.

We must by no means despise the apocalypse. We must keep in mind that its purpose never is to present a scheme of detailed history to be wrought out.   The end of all true prophecy, predictive and declarative, is the same, to serve the moral and spiritual ends of the kingdom of God. Some things are told before they come to pass that when they are come to pass we may believe ; [1] and that we may not stumble where the way seems dark and God's presence in doubt.[2]   To His saints in hours of persecution, and when the prophet may not speak in plain terms on account of peculiar conditions, comes the word of God in apocalypse.[3] So it was in the times of the later Old Testament prophets and so it was when John, Peter and Jude wrote.

We must know the situation of prophet and audience before we can understand the language of

[1] John 15 : 29.   [2] John 16: 1 ff.
[3] Cf. Rev 1 : 9 ff., which explains the form for the whole work.

the cryptogram.   Of one thing we may always be sure ; he meant to teach that God rules, that God cares for what His saints suffer, that they must be faithful to Him under all circumstances, and that in the end righteousness shall reign.[1]   Nothing could be much more surprising than that some most pious and godly men have sought so diligently to find in our Lord's discourses about the destruction of Jerusalem, the consummation of the age and His own appearing, a scheme of history and a plan for material rule, whereas the lessons the Lord Himself pointed are, (1) do not be led astray into expecting to find Christ in the midst of every calamity ; (2) be most faithful in preaching to all nations the Gospel of the kingdom ; (3) be always ready for the coming of your Lord for the time of that coming is not and will not be known.

Here is a warning against being deceived, against being surprised, against neglecting the duty of faithful stewardship with the Master's goods.   On this occasion as on all others Jesus meets questions of curiosity with an insistence on moral earnestness and faithful service.   In other words, He declines to answer questions of this sort which lead men to less concern for the main thing, which is faithful trust and work whatever may be God's times and plans.

[1] See a discriminating article by Rev. R. J. Drummond in *Review and Expositor*, January, 1908, " The Purpose and Forms of New Testament Eschatology."

About this, then, several negative features must be kept in mind:

(1) Jesus declares that of the day and hour of this consummation all men, even He Himself, are in ignorance, the Father only knowing.[1]

(2) That the times and the seasons the Father has reserved to Himself and that it is not for the workers to know them.[2] The full force and application of this statement will be the more evident when we recall the question that called it forth. The followers of Jesus have at last come to understand that Jesus is not seeking to found a great world empire; that their business mainly is a spiritual work and must seek spiritual results. It has been a tedious and unwelcome lesson, but it has been learned. But still they cannot dismiss the Jewish hope of national independence and power. Surely this will be a circumstance attendant on the mission of their Messiah, one result of His incarnation. So they, feeling sure that this is to come now or later, ask Jesus: "Lord, dost Thou at this time restore the kingdom to Israel?" His reply is very significant and bears its force for all workers. He says in effect: "That is a question with which you have nothing to do. Your one business is witnessing to Me and for that you shall have power from My Father."

Some have sought still to know and have justi-

[1] Mark 13:32.　　　　　　　　　　[2] Acts 1:7.

fied themselves by saying that the Spirit later revealed the course of events. appealing to Paul's
word that " faithful Christians are not in darkness
that that day should overtake them as a thief " ; [1]
yet Paul cannot have meant that we are not in ignorance of the time, for he has just said that we
" know perfectly that the Lord cometh as a thief
in the night." Our light is in knowing that He
will come and our protection is constant watchfulness, never falling morally asleep.[2] What Jesus
Himself did not know in the day of His humiliation we shall not do well to seek to know in the
day of our service.

(3) Another thing to be kept in mind is that
Jesus warns against materializing our expectations of His kingdom. To Pilate Jesus declares,
"My kingdom is not of this world," not to be
established by force, He adds : and then declaring
that He is a King He indicates the spiritual character of His kingdom in the words : " To this
end have I been born, and to this end am I come
into the world, that I should bear witness unto
the truth. Every one that is of the truth heareth
My voice." [3] " Being asked by the Pharisees
when the kingdom of God cometh, He answered
them and said, The kingdom of God cometh not
with observation: neither shall they say, Lo,
here ! or there ! for lo, the kingdom of God is
within you." Then He turned from His enemies

[1] 1 Thess. 5 : 4.   [2] 1 Thess. 5 : 1–11.   [3] John 18 : 36 f.

to His friends and warned them against being so eager to see "one of the days of the Son of Man" as to go off after some false suggestion.   There will be no mistake about it when He comes but meantime we are to be in expectant faithfulness.[1]

In all plain statements by our Lord and by His spokesmen the events that are to precede His return, the exact conditions of the world and the outcome of Gospel proclamation, the order of the ages, all are left purposely under such uncertainty as that no man can ever say that they have all now been fulfilled and the day of the Lord is at hand, or that they have not yet all been fulfilled and so the Lord cannot be coming now.   How fully and how long the Gospel is to be preached in all nations; how many people and what social institutions are to be redeemed in this age and what in the next; all this the Father hath set within His own authority and we must work the works of Him that sent our Saviour while the day lasts.[2]

It is possible to elaborate a complete scheme of eschatology only by taking as literal figurative statements and as definite prediction pictorial apocalypse, and then among such figurative and apocalyptic utterances making selections and combining together words by different writers under different circumstances.   At least so it

[1] Luke 17 : 20–37.   [2] John 9 : 4.

appears from examination of many such schemes. There is a rationalism in this process which, while infinitely more reverent than that of the destructive criticism, is equally as serious for sober understanding of the Word of God. If the Bible is a book of riddles it is as little useful for the ordinary reader as if it is a conglomerate of various documents under the hands of many redactors.

But enough of the negative. Let us turn to the clear teaching which has practical bearing on the work of missions. Here we can discuss only a few representative passages. We must take care that so far as possible our passages shall be thoroughly representative and cover all the main facts revealed with reference to the work of missions.

We know that in the seed of Abraham all the families of the earth are to be blessed,[1] and Paul applies this, with almost exclusive force, to Christ and to all who are blessed through Him.[2]

In the covenant promise to the Son "set on the holy hill of Zion" we have already seen how to Him the Father will give the heathen for an inheritance and the uttermost parts of the earth for a possession. The opposing nations He will break with a rod of iron and dash them in pieces like earthen vessels. All the rulers of the earth are invited to submit betimes and accept volun-

[1] Gen. 12 : 1-3.   [2] Gal. 3 : 16.

tarily the service of the Son, to take refuge in Him from His wrath.[1]

Micah presents a picture of the day of grace and peace,[2] a part of which we find also in Isaiah ;[3] Jerusalem is to be in utter desolation on account of iniquity; "But in the latter days it shall come to pass that the mountain of Jehovah's house shall be established at the head of the mountains, and it shall be exalted above the hills ; and peoples shall flow into it. And many nations shall go and say, Come ye, and let us go up unto the mountain of Jehovah, and to the house of the God of Jacob; and He will teach us of His ways and we will walk in His paths. For out of Zion shall go forth instruction, and the word of Jehovah from Jerusalem ; and He will judge among many peoples and will decide concerning strong nations afar off ; and they shall beat their swords into plowshares, and their spears into pruning hooks; nation shall not lift up sword against nation, neither shall they learn war any more." There shall be universal peace with individual rights and possessions. This good time is needed, for now "all the peoples walk every one in the name of his god." But God's Israel will faithfully and persistently walk forever in the name of Jehovah our God until that day. Then the lame and rejected and afflicted peoples shall all

[1] Ps. 2 : 7–12.   [2] Micah 4 : 1–9.   [3] Isa. 2 : 2 ff.

have place and honor in the blessing when "Jehovah will reign over them in Mount Zion from henceforth even forever." Here we see the central and attracting position of the "mountain of Jehovah's house"; the turning to it of peoples and the active efforts of "many nations" to induce men to "go up to the mountain of Jehovah"; the discriminating selection among nations and determination of their part in the movement; the foremost nations shall abolish war and introduce a reign of peace; Jehovah reigning forever over all from Mount Zion.

When we apply this prophecy to the kingdom of the Messiah there comes the temptation to localize and materialize. But Jesus Himself placed a bar to this tendency when He declared to the woman of Samaria that the time was coming in practice, as indeed it was already present in principle, when place worship would be abolished and true worshippers would worship God in spirit and in truth—the wish and aim of God.[1]

The prophet to whom God gave the most vivid pictures of the coming One sees[2] in the midst of the captive degradation of Jehovah's people the messengers of peace and salvation upon the mountains of vision. They proclaim, "Thy God reigneth" and all the watchmen see Jehovah coming back to Jerusalem to comfort and redeem His people manifesting His power

[1] John 4: 21 ff.   [2] Isa. 52: 7–53: 12.

"in the eyes of all the nations ; and all the ends
of the earth have seen the salvation of our God."
There is to be no haste, for Jehovah protects.

But now comes [1] a summary outline of the
Servant's impression on men. He is to prosper
and be exalted and lifted up until He is very
high (verse 13). But meantime He is to be
despised and His claim and mission will astonish
many (verse 14). But as they were at first
astonished at the contrast between appearance
and claim " so shall He startle [2] many nations "
at the revelations of His mission (verse 15). He
will suffer great humiliation and death for His
people, then " He shall see seed, He shall pro-
long His days, and the pleasure of Jehovah shall
prosper in His hands." He shall be satisfied
with the outcome in many made righteous
through the knowledge of Himself. Jehovah
will " divide Him a portion with the great, and
He shall divide the spoil with the strong." [3]

In Isaiah 9 : 6 f. it is said of the Son to be born,
that "the government shall be upon His shoulder " and that " of the increase of His government
and of peace there shall be no end, upon the
throne of David, and upon his kingdom to establish it, and to uphold it with justice and righteousness from henceforth, even forever. The zeal of

[1] Isa. 52 : 13–15.
[2] There can hardly be any question of this rendering.
[3] Isa. 53 : 10–12.

Jehovah of hosts will perform this." The growth of Messiah's kingdom shall be unbroken. With this agree the predictions of Daniel who foresaw that the kingdom "which the God of heaven" set up in the midst of the kings already on the horizon of Daniel's vision "shall never be destroyed, nor shall its sovereignty be left to another people, but it shall break in pieces and consume all those kingdoms, and it shall stand forever." [1] Ultimately "the kingdom and the dominion, and the greatness of the kingdoms under the whole heaven, shall be given to the people of the saints of the Most High ; His kingdom is an everlasting kingdom and all dominions shall serve and obey Him." [2] This is to follow a powerful effort to destroy the saints. In the latter half of Isaiah are many indications of the triumphant conquest of Messiah's rule over all opposition, and of universal recognition of His blessing. In order properly to understand these pledges it is necessary to remember that in these chapters Jehovah's Servant is sometimes personal, the Messiah, sometimes collective, the Messianic people. The Messianic people are called Israel, Jacob, etc., but mean those through whom Jehovah is bringing the blessings of His kingdom to mankind.

One writer bitterly blames those " Christian people" who are so "complacently" given to " ignoring the existence of the Jew " and "appropriating

[1] Dan. 2 : 44.   [2] Dan. 7 : 13 f., 27.

to the Church things and promises which never belonged to it." But it is Paul who bids us, " Know therefore that they that are of faith, these are sons of Abraham. And the Scripture foresee- ing that of faith God justifies the nations an- nounced-beforehand-good-tidings[1] to Abraham, In thee shall all the nations be blessed. So then they who are of faith are blessed with the faithful Abraham . . . that upon the nations the blessing of Abraham might come in Jesus Christ, in order that we may get the promise of the Spirit through faith. . . . For ye are all sons of God through faith in Christ Jesus. . . . Jew nor Greek is possible . . . for all ye are one in Christ Jesus. And if ye are Christ's, then are ye Abraham's seed, and, on the basis of promise, heirs."[2] And Peter applies the term " The Dis- persion," which the Old Testament uses of the scattered people of God, to Christians irrespective of nationality[3] and declares of Christians in gen- eral that they are " an elect race, a royal priest- hood, a holy nation, a people for *God's* own pos- session ; "[4] thus specifically applying to non-Jews the designations formerly supposed to be limited to Israel. This does not at all mean that God has no special plans for " His ancient people," but it does call us to the application of the Messianic

---

[1] One word in the Greek.   [2] Gal. 3 : 7–29.

[3] 1 Peter 1 : 1. The contents of the epistle make it impossible to limit it to Jewish Christians.   [4] 1 Peter 2 : 9 ff.

Scriptures in general to that Israel of God which
is so by faith in Christ Jesus.

Recurring then to the visions of the Evangelical
Isaiah we find in chapter 60 a vivid word picture
of the coming of all peoples to the people of God,
brilliant with the risen Light upon them.   When
all are thus coming eagerly to the brightness of
their rising that nation and kingdom that will not
serve Jehovah's Servant shall perish ; " yea all
those nations shall be utterly wasted " (verse 12).
Similarly, the last word of this prophet [1] is a picture of universal peace and glory, partly wrought
by preaching of the divine glory among the nations and partly by the exercise of God's power
removing and suppressing the incorrigible.

Zechariah has similar visions [2] but with more
elaboration and with the obscurity of apocalypse.

The New Testament would be the proper source
for most definite information as to the progress of
the Gospel age.   Here the striking fact is that
stress is laid on the teaching that this is the age
of " grace and truth," the time for subordinating
all to personal, faithful service of the kingdom of
God, the age of limitless offers of salvation, the
age of the Spirit's power in applying the things
of Christ ; but we do not find much of the details
of eschatological expectation.   It will be better to
outline the certain teachings of prophecy, citing
the New Testament passages as they apply.

[1] Isa. 66.   [2] Especially Chs. 8, 9, 13.

These will of course be in harmony with, and interpretative of, the Old Testament predictions.

(1) Jesus announced a kingdom that is to be all embracing and final.[1] This is assumed by Him and accepted by His hearers in a way that requires little affirmation. His Church shall never be overcome by the powers of Hades and the keys of the kingdom shall be forever admitting such as are being saved.[2] On this point no question seems ever to have entered the minds of His Apostles. "The kingdom of our Lord and Saviour Jesus Christ" is "eternal." That kingdom is now present but is incomplete and awaits its glory.[3] It needs not to be sought after for it is already among and within men,[4] men are now pressing into it.[5]

(2) His kingdom is to be on earth but is essentially spiritual and we must beware of materializing it. The kingdom of God is not meat and drink but righteousness, peace and joy in the Holy Spirit.[6] Flesh and blood cannot inherit it, nor any corruptible element.[7] So that in a certain—the full—sense we shall not enter it until delivered from this life.[8]

(3) This kingdom is to be progressive. It will grow steadily wider and deeper, gaining in-

---

[1] Cf. Matt. 28 : 18-20.   [2] Cf. Matt. 16 : 16 ff. ; Acts 2 : 47.
[3] Matt. 16 : 27 f. ; 1 Thess 2 : 12, etc.   [4] Luke 17 : 21.
[5] Matt. 11 : 12.   [6] Rom. 14 : 17.
[7] 1 Cor. 15 : 50.   [8] 2 Tim. 4 : 18.

creasing hold on men, increasing power in the earth, increasing influence with the rulers of men.[1] The kingdoms of this world shall become the kingdom of our Lord and His Messiah.[2] So the parables of the leaven, the mustard seed, the seed growing of itself, the king going into a far country to receive his kingdom. The "little flock" with which He begins are to have no fear for it is the Father's good pleasure to give them the kingdom.[3] The kingdom which has been given Him of the Father He gives to them.

(4) In exact accord with the Old Testament presentations, we find that Jesus had no expectation of gaining all men to willing and loyal submission. He entertained no false optimism, He had no delusion about the depth and bitter persistence of human rebellion against His Father He found in His own experience how many there were who would not come unto Him that they might have life. His heart must bleed in compassionate pity over them that He would save while they would not.[4] If they had rejected Him they would reject His messengers also; but as some had received His word so also would they receive that of His servants.[5]

The words with which Jesus spoke to the disciples on the evening of the close of His

---

[1] Luke 1 : 32 f. ; cf. Dan. 2 : 44, etc.; Isa. 9 : 7.
[2] Rev. 11 : 15.   [3] Luke 12 : 32.
[4] Matt. 23 : 37 ; cf. John 5 : 40.   [5] John 15 : 17 ff.

ministry[1] show clearly how fully He realized that He was kindling a fire in the earth that must burn many, sending a sword among men. The Gospel could not be a savor of life unto life without being a savor of death unto death.[2]

A number of passages in the Gospels and Pastoral Epistles, and some elsewhere, indicate a period, or periods of "falling away"[3] and of great wickedness attending the progress of the kingdom. That such should be the case belongs to the very nature of men and of spiritual things. Of course such "falling away" will be antecedent to the glorious fullness of the kingdom. That there is to be some very special and unique manifestation is also affirmed but its nature can hardly be known before the event. What Paul refers to in Thessalonians[4] was already incipient in his time. That the forces of evil will prove especially malignant is to be expected at various stages. "Evil men and impostors will wax worse and worse"[5] but that is not to say that they will be in preponderate numbers or in triumphant position. "They shall not proceed too far"[6] being under the limitations of God who maketh the wrath of men to praise Him while the remainder of wrath He doth restrain.[7]

---

[1] Matt. 24–25; Mark 13; Luke 19.   [2] 2 Cor. 2 : 16.
[3] Cf. 1 Tim. 4 : 1 ff.; 2 Tim. 3 : 1, and the apocalyptic discourse of Jesus, as above.   [4] 2 Thess. 2.
[5] 2 Tim. 3 : 13.   [6] 2 Tim. 3 : 9.   [7] Ps. 76 : 10.

The fact of intense and extensive hindrance to the progress of religion of Jesus; in spite of the fact that the love of many will grow cold and lampstands are frequently removed because their light has failed; there still seems to be no proof that Jesus or His Apostles expected any cessation of the progressive development of the truth and the salvation of God in the earth until the time shall come for closing the missionary age.

(5) There is to be a restoration of the Jewish people, even of the whole Hebrew people, to "saving favor." So we usually phrase it. Perhaps we should say they are to come to a receptive attitude to the Messiah. Here the details are uncertain. Paul gives us the most distinct New Testament teaching on this subject in Romans 9–11. After expressing his own deep longing and grief over "his brethren" he insists that their unbelief does not argue that "the word of God hath come to nought,"[1] for natural relation is not the basis of determination; "it is not the children of the flesh that are children of God"[2] and "they are not all Israel that are of Israel."[3] God endured for long "vessels fitted for destruction" and displays the riches of His glory upon "vessels of mercy, which He afore prepared unto glory, whom He also called, not from the Jews only, but also from the Gentiles."[4] It

[1] Rom. 9: 6.
[2] Rom. 9: 6.
[3] Rom. 9: 8.
[4] Rom. 9: 22f.

is not at all a matter of race but of grace and of accepting the divine call, and this is God's purpose as announced through Hosea [1] and Isaiah.[2] He then shows, in chapter 11, that, lacking faith, the natural Israel has in the past not been saved. Has God then cast away His people?[3] Not at all, many of them are saved, Paul himself being an example. There is "a remnant according to the election of grace" (verse 5) that is saved but not on the basis of formal work or of lineage. The trespass and rejection of the Jews is based on their unbelief; the acceptance and salvation of the Gentiles is by God's grace through faith. This Jewish apostasy is partial and temporary.[4] Then, in a pregnant passage [5] we read this remarkable outline: "For I do not wish you to be ignorant, brethren, as to this secret—so that you may not be wise in your own conceits—that a condition of hardness in part has come upon Israel until the time when the fullness of the Gentiles (the complete recognition of the principle of the salvation of the nations) come in; and thus all Israel will be saved, even as it is written:

There shall come out of Zion the Deliverer;

And He shall turn away ungodliness from Jacob;

And this is the covenant which I give them, [6]

---

[1] Hosea 2 : 23; cf. 1 : 10.

[2] Isa. 10 : 22f.; cf. 1 : 9.

[3] Rom. 11 : 1.

[4] Rom. 11 : 7-24.

[5] Verses 25-32.

[6] From Isa. 59 : 20f.

Whenever I shall take away their sins.[1]

On the basis of the Gospel, then, they are enemies through you, but on the basis of the election they are beloved through the fathers; for not to be regretted are the gifts and the calling of God. For just as you were formerly disobedient to God, and now were shown mercy in their disobedience, even so were these for the present disobedient in your mercy (time) in order that they too may now have mercy. For God did shut them all up together into disobedience in order that He might be merciful unto them all."

The rejection of the Messiah by the Jews, as their historical rejection of Jehovah even before the Messiah's advent, and God's rejection of them was the occasion of reconciling the world, and their restoration will be life from the dead (verse 15). God has put all men on a common basis under the Gospel; all are in disobedience and death, all are offered life through faith.[2] Israel is dear to God's heart because of His past relations to them: the root is holy and so must the branches be; the first fruit (the many early Jewish converts) is holy and betokens a holy harvest in its time.[3] That this means that the Jews are to be the special agents of evangelization is not so clear though for Semitic peoples they would seem the fitting missionaries and the Semitic peoples have so far been

[1] From Isa. 27 : 9.   [2] Cf. the argument in Rom. 1–3.
[3] Rom. 11 : 16.

little reached by Gentile missionaries. That Gentile Christians are all to be removed from the world while Jews carry the Gospel seems an unfounded fancy of the scheme building brethren. That the Jews are to have another period of national life and prosperity seems to be predicted but we cannot forget that God's promises are conditional to the nations, and that there is great danger of material literalness in interpreting the predictions of a Faith that is concerned primarily with the spirit. Certain it is that much of the agitation of this subject in our own time, as heretofore, is along lines calculated to engender in the Jews just such earthly, material and sordid hopes as proved their undoing when the Messiah came two thousand years ago, and when the splendor of a glorious earthly kingdom in their hopes blinded their eyes to their King coming to them with justice and salvation, lowly and riding upon an ass.[1] Whatever may be in store for Israel in earthly rule we may feel quite sure that God is far more desirous of leading them into the spiritual kingdom of redeeming love than to an earthly Canaan of material and temporal splendor. And in this leading we may have a share; the other God must work by His own counsels.

With the jealousy of those who so covet for Christ a great earthly dominion for a period of a thousand years when men yield a feigned obedi-

[1] Zech. 9: 9.

ence, under material force, supporting the expectation by literal reading of apocalyptic utterance, we cannot go while we remember that Jesus would not allow men to make Him a king; that He declared that His kingdom is not of this world, and that He rebuked the disciples who at the last moment sought to know whether the kingdom might not now be restored to Israel.

(6) In the end Christ will triumph over all opposition and will reign supreme in a spiritual world and "then the end when He shall deliver up the kingdom to the God and Father; when He shall have abolished all rule and all authority and power. For He must reign till He hath put all His enemies under His feet. . . And when all things have been subjected unto Him, then shall the Son also Himself be subjected to Him that did subject all things unto Him, that God may be all in all."[1] God's plan is, in the administering of "the fullness of the times, to sum up all things in Christ, the things upon the heavens and the things upon the earth."[2] Because of the obedient humiliation of Christ Jesus "God highly exalted Him, and gave unto Him the name which is above every name; that in the name Jesus every knee shall bow, of things in heaven, in earth and under the earth, and that every tongue shall confess that Jesus Christ is Lord unto the glory of God the

[1] I Cor 15: 24-28.　　　[2] Eph. 1: 10; cf. Col. 1: 16-20.

Father." [1]   That the final submission of many
men and institutions must be compulsory,
before " the earth shall be full of the knowledge of Jehovah, as the waters cover the sea," [2]
we are left in no doubt, but the exact nature
of this power and its application we cannot
conclude from the figures of wars and natural
calamities which picture the awful facts. That
the work of missions saves multitudes from wrath
is clear and the long-suffering delay of God
means salvation. [3]

(7) In the face of all this prophecy the
Christian duty faithfully to bear witness to
Jesus as Saviour is unaffected by any plans
which God may hold within His own authority,
save in so far as a knowledge of the holding of
such plans adds seriousness and hope, conviction and joy to the acceptance of that
duty.

We know that Jesus Christ is the propitiation
for our sins and for the whole world ; that the
whole world lieth in the wicked one; that this
is life eternal, that they should know the Father
as the only true God, and Jesus Christ as the
one whom He hath sent ; that He sends us
into the world to proclaim salvation to all ;
that some will reject us with His message
as they rejected Him ; that as He will not,

[1] Phil. 2: 9-11, literal.   [2] Isa. 11: 9.
[3] Cf. 2 Peter 3: 9 ; Rom. 2: 4.

neither shall we fail nor be discouraged till He shall have set justice in the earth and the isles shall wait for His law; that the dispensation of the ages with their "times and seasons" are in the authority and control of the Father who administers them with reference to redemption through the Gospel; that it is ours to go right on working to the utmost, in the manner and with the means of our commission, to establish the kingdom of God in the earth : that in it all our Lord and we, through His Holy Spirit, work for certain success, forasmuch as we know that our labor is not in vain in the Lord.

In God's time and way, partly by our faithful efforts,

> " Jesus shall reign, where'er the Sun
> Does his successive journeys run,
> His kingdom spread from shore to shore,
> Till moons shall wax and wane no more."

Even so, Come, Lord Jesus !   Amen !

INDEX